Hedge Funds

Foundations and Frameworks Series

An Introduction to Alternative Investments & Absolute Return Strategies

Elian Vale

TME Press email: support@tme.net

Introduction

In 1949, a sociologist named Alfred Winslow Jones did something strange with his own money. He bought stocks he thought would rise, and at the same time he bet against stocks he thought would fall. Then he borrowed money to make both bets bigger. Most investors at the time thought he had lost his mind. Why hold two positions that seemed to cancel each other out? But Jones understood something that the rest of Wall Street had missed. By owning good companies and shorting bad ones, he could make money whether the overall market went up or down. He had "hedged" his risk. The fund he built went on to beat the best mutual funds of its era by a wide margin, and when a journalist finally wrote about him in 1966, everyone wanted to know how he did it. That structure Jones stumbled into became the blueprint for a multi-trillion-dollar industry.

This book is about that industry and the broader world it belongs to. Hedge funds are one part of a category called alternative investments, which includes anything that falls outside traditional stocks, bonds, and cash. The people who run these funds chase a goal called absolute return, which means making money in good years and bad ones rather than simply beating a benchmark. It sounds simple when you put it that way. In practice, the strategies used to get there can be complex, the fee structures can be steep, and the risks can be real. That is exactly why this book exists. You will learn how these funds actually work, what separates the good ones from the dangerous ones, and how large institutions decide where to put their money.

Here is a fair warning before you go further. Alternative investments have a reputation for being intimidating. The jargon is thick. The math can get heavy. Fund managers sometimes seem to speak a private language designed to keep outsiders confused. This book takes the opposite approach. Every concept is explained in plain terms, with real examples wherever they help. You don't need a finance degree to follow along. You need curiosity and a willingness to think carefully. If you have those, you are ready.

Let's talk about who this book is for. Maybe you work in finance and want to understand a corner of it you have never touched. Maybe you're a student trying to figure out whether this career path suits you. Maybe you sit on the board of a foundation or an endowment and you keep hearing about hedge fund allocations you are expected to vote on. Or maybe you are an individual investor who has grown curious about what wealthy families and big institutions do with their money that you cannot. All of these readers will find something useful here. The book assumes you know the basics of investing, such as what a stock is and how a bond pays interest, but it doesn't assume anything beyond that.

Now for the structure, so you know what road you are on.

The book opens by answering a deceptively simple question: what actually makes an investment "alternative"? Chapter 1 draws the line between traditional and alternative assets, explains the difference between chasing absolute return and beating a benchmark, and covers the rules about who is even allowed to invest in these funds. You will learn why certain investments lock up your money for years and why regulators treat these funds so differently from the mutual fund you might hold in a retirement account.

Chapter 2 pulls back the curtain on the hedge fund business itself. This is where you learn about the famous "2 and 20" fee structure, which means a fund charges 2 percent of your money each year plus 20 percent of any profits it generates. You will see how high-water marks protect investors from paying twice for the same gains, and why some funds set up shop in places like the Cayman Islands. Understanding the business model matters because fees quietly eat into returns, and knowing how the manager gets paid tells you a lot about whether their interests line up with yours.

From there the book moves into specific strategies, and this is where things get interesting. Chapter 3 covers long/short equity, the approach Alfred Jones invented. You will learn how managers pick stocks to buy and stocks to bet against, what it means to be "market neutral," and how activist investors buy big stakes in companies and push for change. Chapter 4 explores global macro and managed futures, where traders bet on the direction of entire economies, currencies, and interest rates. Some do this through gut instinct and deep research. Others build computer systems that follow trends automatically, with no human making the individual calls.

Chapter 5 gets into event-driven and relative value strategies, which sound abstract but are actually quite concrete. When two companies announce a merger, a gap usually opens between the stock price and the agreed deal price. Merger arbitrage funds try to capture that gap. When a company goes bankrupt, distressed debt investors buy its bonds for cents on the dollar and bet on a recovery. These strategies profit from specific events rather than broad market moves.

Chapter 6 turns to the quants, the funds run largely by mathematicians and programmers. You will learn about statistical arbitrage, factor investing, and the growing role of machine learning in building portfolios. This chapter also covers a trap that catches many beginners: a strategy can look brilliant when tested against past data and then fall apart in the real world. Knowing why that happens will make you a sharper judge of any track record you are shown.

Then the book shifts from offense to defense. Chapter 7 is about risk management, which is arguably the part that separates funds that survive from funds that blow up. You will learn how managers measure their potential losses, how leverage magnifies both gains and disasters, and why correlations between assets tend to break down at the worst possible moment. History is full of funds that looked unstoppable right up until they weren't, and most of those stories trace back to risk that was poorly understood or ignored.

Chapter 8 teaches you how to evaluate a fund before handing over a single dollar. This is called due diligence, and it covers far more than past performance. You will learn to spot survivorship bias, which is the illusion created when failed funds quietly disappear from the records and only the winners remain visible. You'll get a practical checklist for examining a fund's operations, its terms, and the people running it.

Reference checks and background verification matter more than most realize, and this chapter shows you why.

The book closes with Chapter 9, which zooms out to how the biggest players think. Foundations, university endowments, and pension funds allocate enormous sums to alternatives, and they do it with a discipline most individuals never see. You will learn about the Yale endowment model, which reshaped how institutions invest, along with how these organizations balance the desire for high returns against the need to keep some money liquid and available. This chapter ties everything together by showing how the strategies from earlier in the book fit into a full portfolio.

After the final chapter, you will find several sections built to make this book genuinely useful long after you finish reading.

There is a Conclusion that pulls the main threads together. There are Example Answers to the End-of-Chapter Questions, so you can test yourself and check your thinking as you go. A Historical Timeline of Hedge Funds gives you the major events and turning points in one place, from Alfred Jones through the modern era. An Interview Guide to Hedge Funds Across Investment Styles helps you understand how professionals in each strategy actually talk about their work, which is valuable whether you're preparing for a job or simply trying to sound informed in a meeting. A Key Terms and Definitions section serves as your quick reference for the vocabulary, so you never have to guess what a word means. Finally, Works Cited and Recommended Readings points you toward the best sources if you want to go deeper on any topic.

So what will you actually walk away with? A few things. You'll understand how alternative investments work and why people pay so much to access them. You will be able to tell the difference between a strategy that makes sense and one that is dressed-up gambling. You'll know what questions to ask before trusting anyone with money, and you will recognize the warning signs that experienced investors watch for. Most of all, you will lose the sense that this world is closed off to you. The concepts are learnable.

A quick note on how to read this book. The chapters build on each other, so reading in order works best the first time through. That said, each chapter stands on its own well enough that you can jump to a specific strategy if that is what you need. The end-of-chapter questions are worth doing rather than skipping. Writing out an answer forces you to notice the gaps in your understanding, and the example answers in the back let you check your work.

Alfred Jones didn't set out to launch an industry. He was a curious individual testing an idea with his own savings. That spirit, careful thinking paired with a willingness to question how things are normally done, runs through the best investors in this field. By the end of this book, you will understand their world well enough to form your own opinions about it. Turn the page and let's begin.

Outline

Contents

Chapter 1: What Makes an Investment "Alternative"

The word "alternative" is a strange way to define an entire category of investing. It tells you what these assets aren't, not what they are. Stocks, bonds, and cash sit at the center of the financial universe, and almost everything else gets swept into one catch-all bucket, as if the only thing a soybean futures contract and a stake in a private software company have in common is that neither one is a share of Apple.

That vagueness causes real confusion. People hear "alternative investment" and picture something exotic and slightly disreputable, or they assume it's a single product they can buy. It's neither. The category covers hedge funds, private equity, venture capital, real estate, commodities, private credit, farmland, timber, fine art, and a dozen other things. What ties them together isn't a shared strategy. It's a shared set of characteristics: they mostly trade outside public exchanges, they answer to lighter regulation, they're harder to buy and sell, and they're usually walled off from ordinary investors by law.

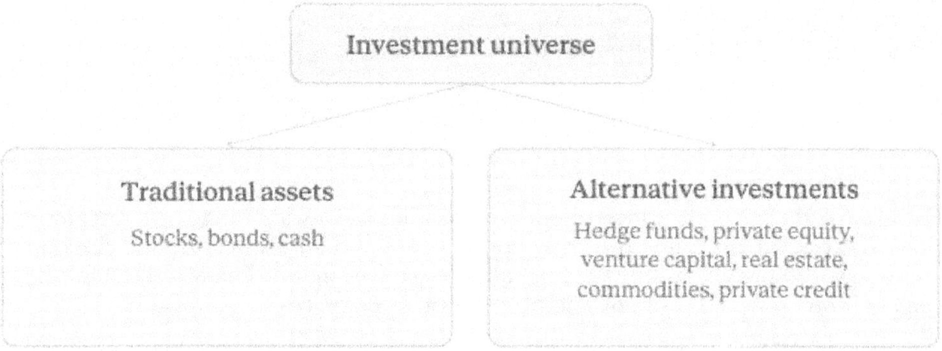

Attribute	Traditional	Alternative
Liquidity	Daily	Locked up, years
Regulation	Heavy	Light
Transparency	Public disclosure	Limited disclosure
Pricing	Continuous	Periodic estimate
Access	Open to all	Accredited only

This chapter is about those characteristics, because once you understand them, the whole field stops looking like a random collection of products and starts making sense as a coherent way of thinking about money.

Defining Traditional vs. Alternative Asset Classes

Start with what "traditional" means, because you can't define the exception without the rule.

Traditional assets are the three things almost every investor already owns in some form: publicly traded stocks, publicly traded bonds, and cash or cash equivalents like money market funds and Treasury bills.

When your employer sets up a retirement account, these are the building blocks inside it. They're traditional for good reasons. You can buy them in seconds through any brokerage app. You can sell them just as fast. Their prices update constantly and publicly, so you always know what your holdings are worth. And they sit under decades of regulation designed to protect people who don't read prospectuses.

Alternative assets break at least one of those rules, usually several at once. A private equity fund that buys whole companies can't be sold with a tap on your phone. A piece of farmland doesn't have a ticker symbol or a price that refreshes every second. A hedge fund won't tell the public what it owns. Once you notice this, the category clarifies itself. An asset is "alternative" when it lives outside the fast, transparent, heavily regulated domain of public markets.

It helps to walk through the main types, because "alternative" is an umbrella and the things underneath it behave very differently.

Hedge funds are pooled investment vehicles that use a wide range of strategies to chase returns, often trading the same public stocks and bonds as everyone else but doing so with borrowing, short selling, and derivatives that ordinary mutual funds can't or won't touch. This book spends most of its pages here.

Private equity funds buy controlling stakes in private companies, or take public companies private, then try to improve them over several years before selling at a profit. When a firm like Blackstone or KKR buys a chain of restaurants, improves its operations, and sells it five years later, that's private equity at work.

Venture capital is a cousin of private equity focused on young companies. When a fund writes an early check to a startup that later becomes Uber or Airbnb, the returns can be enormous, but most startups fail, so the model depends on a few huge winners covering many losers.

Real assets cover things you can physically point to: commercial real estate, infrastructure like toll roads and pipelines, farmland, and timberland. These generate income and tend to hold value when inflation rises, which is part of why large investors like them.

Commodities include oil, natural gas, gold, copper, wheat, and the like, usually held through futures contracts rather than physical barrels or bushels.

Collectibles and private credit round out the far edges: fine art, rare wine, classic cars, and the growing business of lending money directly to companies outside the banking system.

The differences between these matter, but the family resemblance matters more. Here's a side-by-side comparison of the two broad categories on the features that actually separate them.

Feature	Traditional Assets	Alternative Assets
Where they trade	Public exchanges	Private markets, direct deals
Liquidity	High, sell in seconds to days	Low, often locked up for months or years
Pricing	Continuous and public	Periodic, often by appraisal or estimate
Regulation	Heavy, extensive disclosure	Lighter, limited disclosure
Who can invest	Nearly anyone	Wealthy and institutional investors only
Typical fees	Low, often under 1%	High, often 1-2% plus a share of profits
Correlation to stock market	High by definition	Often lower, sometimes much lower

That last row deserves attention, because it's the reason sophisticated investors bother with alternatives at all. Correlation measures how closely two things move together. If everything you own rises and falls in lockstep, you haven't spread your risk, you've just multiplied one bet. The appeal of many alternatives is that they don't move in perfect time with the stock market. When public stocks crashed in 2008, some hedge fund strategies still made money, and certain real assets kept producing economic returns (and not "holding their value" simply because they're illiquid). An investor who owned only stocks felt the full blow. An investor who'd spread money across assets that behaved differently felt a softer one.

I want to flag something honest here, because the diversification story gets oversold. The low-correlation benefit is real, but it's not constant. In the worst moments of a crisis, correlations across almost everything tend to spike toward one, meaning things that normally move independently suddenly fall together as panicked investors sell whatever they can. The very moment you most want your alternatives to hold steady is sometimes the moment they don't. This doesn't erase the benefit. It just means the benefit is conditional, and anyone who promises you that alternatives will always cushion a downturn is selling a fantasy.

There's also a question of valuation that trips up newcomers. When you own a public stock, its price is whatever the market says at this second, and there's no arguing with it. When you own a stake in a private company or a hedge fund holding hard-to-price positions, the value is often an estimate, produced quarterly, sometimes by the fund manager's own model. This creates a subtle illusion. Private assets look less volatile than public ones partly because they're priced less often. A building's market value swings just as much as a stock's, but if you only get an appraisal once a year, you never see the swings, so the investment feels calmer than it really is. Some investors even prefer alternatives for this reason, valuing the smoother-looking ride even though the underlying risk hasn't changed. That preference is understandable and a little irrational, and it's worth being aware of in yourself.

The Absolute Return Objective vs. Relative Return Benchmarks

Here's a scenario that captures the entire philosophical divide in professional investing.

A mutual fund manager runs a fund benchmarked to the S&P 500. In a brutal year, the S&P falls 20 percent. Her fund falls only 15 percent. She sends her investors a letter noting that the fund beat its benchmark by five full percentage points, and she collects her bonus for a job well done. Her investors, meanwhile, are looking at accounts worth 15 percent less than they were in January. The manager celebrated a win. The investors lost money. Both are correct about what happened, and the gap between their reactions is the difference between relative return and absolute return.

Relative return is the standard by which most of the investment industry measures itself. A manager picks a benchmark, usually a market index, and success means beating it. Trail the index and you've failed, even if you made money. Beat the index and you've succeeded, even if your investors lost a fortune. This isn't as absurd as it sounds. Index funds are cheap and easy to buy, so if you're paying a manager to do better than an index, it's fair to judge whether they actually did. The logic holds. It just produces the uncomfortable result that a manager can win in a year her clients lost real money.

Absolute return flips the goal. An absolute return strategy aims to make positive money regardless of what the broader market does. The target isn't "beat the S&P 500." The target is "don't lose money, and ideally earn a steady positive return whether stocks are soaring or collapsing." A fund earning six percent in a year the market fell 20 percent has done its job perfectly, even though it trailed no index because it wasn't trying to track one.

Relative return	Absolute return
Market falls 20 percent	Market falls 20 percent
Fund return: negative 15 percent	Fund return: positive 6 percent
Benchmark: S&P 500, negative 20 percent	Target: cash rate plus 5 percent
Result: 5 points ahead of benchmark	Result: 1 point ahead of target
Manager collects her bonus	Tracked no index at all
Verdict: manager wins	**Verdict: manager wins**
Investor is down 15 percent	Investor is up 6 percent

Same market, two definitions of winning

This is the promise that built the hedge fund industry. The pitch is seductive: put your money with us and we'll grow it in good times and protect it in bad ones, smoothing out the terror of market crashes. Foundations, pension funds, and wealthy families found that idea worth paying handsomely for, which is how the famous "2 and 20" fee structure survived so long.

Now the honest part, because this book won't sell you the pitch without the fine print.

Very few hedge funds actually deliver pure absolute return. True market neutrality, where a fund's results have no connection to the stock market's direction, is genuinely hard to achieve and rare in practice. Most funds that call themselves absolute return still carry some exposure to the market, so when stocks fall hard, they usually fall too, just less. And the flip side of the promise is the part managers mention quietly: in strong bull markets, absolute return strategies often lag badly. During the long rally of the 2010s, a plain S&P 500 index fund that charged almost nothing outperformed the large majority of hedge funds charging 2 and 20. Investors noticed. Warren Buffett famously bet a hedge fund firm a large sum that a simple index fund would beat a basket of hedge funds over ten years, and he won handily. The episode became a rallying point for critics who argue that the absolute return promise is worth less than its price.

So who's right? Both camps have a point, and the resolution depends on what you actually want. If you want the highest possible return over decades and you can stomach gut-wrenching drawdowns along the way, a cheap stock index fund is tough to beat. If you're a pension fund that must pay retirees every month and can't afford to lose 40 percent in a single bad year, a strategy that gives up some upside in exchange for smaller losses (e.g., because it's hedging prudently against bad drawdowns and thus incurs costs) might be worth every penny of its fees, because avoiding a catastrophic drawdown matters more to you than squeezing out the last point of return. The absolute return objective isn't better or worse than relative return. It serves a different need.

Because the two mindsets measure success so differently, it's worth laying them side by side.

Dimension	Relative Return	Absolute Return
Goal	Beat a chosen benchmark	Earn positive returns in any market
A "good year"	Trailing benchmark by less, even at a loss	Making money regardless of the market
Typical vehicle	Mutual funds, index funds, ETFs	Hedge funds, some managed futures
Benchmark used	Market index like the S&P 500	Cash rate plus a spread, or simply zero
Behavior in a crash	Falls with the market, hopes to fall less	Aims to protect capital or profit
Behavior in a boom	Rises with the market	Often lags the market's gains
Fee model	Low, mostly flat	High, flat fee plus profit share

Notice the benchmark row. Absolute return funds often measure themselves against a cash rate plus a margin, something like "the Treasury bill rate plus five percent." The reasoning is that an investor could always just hold cash safely, so a fund should be judged on how much it earns above that risk-free baseline. When short-term interest rates were near zero for much of the 2010s, clearing that bar looked easy. When rates climbed above five percent in 2023, the same funds suddenly had to work much harder to justify themselves, because cash alone was paying a respectable return with no risk at all. The bar moves with the wider economy, and a fund that looked brilliant in a zero-rate world can look ordinary when safe cash competes with it.

Illiquidity Premium and Lock-Up Structures

Suppose two investments offer the same expected return. One lets you pull your money out any day you like. The other locks it away for three years, no exceptions, no early exit. Which would you choose?

Almost everyone picks the flexible one, and that instinct is the whole basis for the illiquidity premium. If a locked-up investment offered no more reward than a liquid one, nobody rational would accept the lock-up. So illiquid investments have to pay you extra to compensate for the freedom you're giving up. That extra expected return, the reward for tying up your money, is the illiquidity premium. It's one of the central reasons alternatives can, in theory, earn more than public markets.

The theory is sound and the premium appears to be real, especially in private equity and venture capital, where money routinely gets locked away for a decade. Investors in those funds have historically earned returns above public stocks, and a good chunk of that edge is thought to be payment for illiquidity. But the word "premium" makes it sound guaranteed, and it isn't. You're being compensated for accepting a real constraint, and the compensation only materializes if the manager actually delivers. Plenty of illiquid funds have locked up investor money for years and then produced mediocre or terrible results. In those cases the investor got the lock-up without the premium, which is the worst of both worlds. Illiquidity is a cost you accept in hope of a reward, not a reward in itself.

Hedge funds manage this constraint through a set of contractual mechanisms, and you need to understand them before you ever wire money to one, because they determine whether you can actually get your cash back when you want it.

The **lock-up period** is the initial stretch after you invest during which you simply can't withdraw, period. One year is common. Some funds impose two or three. The manager wants this so she can invest with a longer horizon without worrying that a nervous investor will yank money out at the first dip, forcing her to sell good positions at bad prices.

After the lock-up expires, you still can't withdraw whenever you feel like it. Funds only allow redemptions on a schedule, often quarterly or annually, and you have to give **advance notice**, typically 30 to 90 days. So even a fund that's technically "open" to withdrawals might mean that if you decide today you want out, you file notice now and see your money three or four months from now, at the next scheduled window. That lag can feel agonizing when markets are falling and you desperately want your capital in hand.

Then come the defensive tools that funds deploy when many investors try to leave at once. A **gate** limits total withdrawals in any single period, often capping them at 25 percent of the fund's assets per quarter. If too many people ask for their money simultaneously, the gate comes down and everyone gets only a fraction of what they requested, with the rest paid out later. A **side pocket** segregates hard-to-sell positions into a separate account so that investors redeeming from the main fund can't force a fire-sale of assets that need time to unwind.

These mechanisms sound reasonable on paper, and they exist for a defensible reason: they protect the fund and its remaining investors from a stampede that would destroy value for everyone. Then 2008 arrived and showed the world what they feel like in practice. As markets cratered, hedge funds across the industry slammed their gates shut and suspended redemptions. Investors who wanted out, who needed their cash, who were watching their net worth evaporate, simply couldn't get their money. It sat trapped inside funds for months, sometimes longer. The experience was traumatic and it permanently changed how investors think about liquidity terms. The lesson wasn't that gates and lock-ups are terrible in and of themselves. It was that they're real, they bite hardest exactly when you least want them to, and you must understand them fully before investing, not discover them during a crisis.

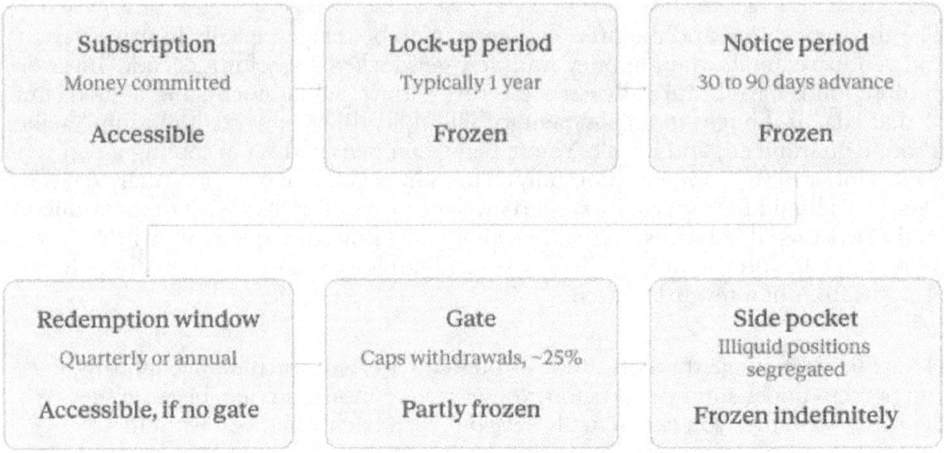

These terms protect the fund; they bite hardest in a crisis

This is the practical wisdom around illiquidity: match the lock-up to money you genuinely won't need. Endowments and pension funds handle long lock-ups well because their obligations stretch across decades and they can plan around a portion of their assets being frozen. An individual who might need cash for a medical bill or a job loss has no business locking up money they can't afford to lose access to, no matter how attractive the promised premium. The illiquidity premium is only worth capturing with money you can truly afford to leave alone.

Accredited and Qualified Investor Requirements

Here's something that surprises people when they first learn it: most of the investments in this book are illegal for the average person to buy. Not frowned upon. Not risky. Legally off-limits. The government has decided that ordinary investors aren't allowed to put money into most hedge funds and private funds, and understanding why reveals a lot about how these markets work.

The reasoning traces back to a bargain baked into securities law. Public investments come wrapped in heavy disclosure requirements, audited filings, and regulatory oversight, all of it meant to protect people who can't fend for themselves. Private funds are exempt from most of that. In exchange for the lighter rules, they're only allowed to take money from investors the law presumes can handle the risk on their own, either because they're wealthy enough to absorb a total loss or sophisticated enough to evaluate what they're getting into. The wealth thresholds are a rough proxy for that presumed sophistication. They're imperfect, and critics attack them constantly, but they're the line the system draws.

The first and lower bar is the **accredited investor** standard. An individual qualifies by clearing any one of a few tests. On wealth, you need a net worth above one million dollars, not counting the value of your primary residence, held either alone or together with a spouse. On income, you need to have earned more than 200,000 dollars in each of the past two years, or 300,000 jointly with a spouse, with a reasonable expectation of the same this year. In 2020, regulators added a third path that doesn't depend on money at all: holding certain financial licenses in good standing, specifically the Series 7, Series 65, or Series 82, now qualifies you regardless of your net worth. That change was small but meaningful, because it was the first crack in the idea that only wealth can signal sophistication.

The higher bar is the **qualified purchaser** standard, and it's a much steeper climb. To qualify, an individual generally needs at least five million dollars in investments, a figure that pointedly excludes your home and counts only actual investable assets. Entities face an even higher threshold. This tier exists because certain funds, the ones that want to accept an unlimited number of investors, are only permitted to take money from qualified purchasers. The law essentially says that if a fund wants fewer restrictions on how many people it can serve, every one of those people has to be seriously wealthy.

The gap between these two standards matters, so here's the comparison directly.

Standard	Individual Threshold	What It Unlocks
Accredited investor	$1M net worth excluding home, or $200K income ($300K joint), or certain securities licenses	Access to most private funds under the 100-investor limit
Qualified purchaser	$5M in investments (individuals); $25M for most entities	Access to funds that accept unlimited qualified investors

There's a quieter third label worth a mention, the **qualified client**, which governs whether a fund can even charge you a performance fee. That share of profits at the heart of the hedge fund model isn't something a manager can legally collect from just anyone. Under the rules, you generally need either a certain amount of money invested with the manager or a net worth above a set threshold, both of which get adjusted for inflation over time. The practical effect is that the people paying performance fees are, by law, a wealthy subset to begin with.

All of this fuels a genuine and unresolved debate. Defenders of these rules argue they protect unsophisticated people from complex, illiquid, lightly regulated products they might not understand, products that can and do wipe out investors. Critics counter that the rules are backward and unfair: the highest-returning investments get reserved for people who are already rich, so the wealthy compound their advantage while everyone else is locked into public markets, and wealth gets treated as a stand-in for intelligence when the two clearly aren't the same thing. Both sides land real punches. A schoolteacher with a doctorate in finance can't invest in a fund that will happily take money from a lottery winner who can't read a balance sheet. The system is coarse. It's also the system, and if you want to participate in this field, knowing exactly which door you're allowed through is the starting point.

Regulatory Framework: The 1940 Act and Private Fund Exemptions

Every structural feature this chapter has covered, the lock-ups, the wealth requirements, the secrecy about holdings, traces back to a single foundational law and the clever ways funds arrange themselves to sidestep it. To understand why hedge funds look the way they do, you have to understand what they're avoiding.

The law is the **Investment Company Act of 1940**, passed in the aftermath of the 1929 crash and the abuses that came with it. It governs "investment companies," which is the legal term for pooled vehicles that invest on behalf of many people, the category that includes mutual funds. The Act is strict by design. It caps how much a fund can borrow, forces regular public disclosure of holdings, limits fees, requires independent directors, restricts transactions with insiders, and demands that funds let investors redeem their shares on short notice. These rules are why mutual funds are as safe and transparent as they are. They're also why mutual funds can't do most of what hedge funds do. A fund bound by the 1940 Act simply can't borrow aggressively, sell short without limit, or lock up investor money for years.

So hedge funds don't play by those rules. They arrange themselves to fall outside the definition of an "investment company" entirely, which frees them from the Act's constraints. They do this by fitting into one of two exemptions, and nearly every hedge fund in America relies on one of them.

The first is **Section 3(c)(1)**. A fund qualifies for this exemption by keeping its number of investors at or below 100 and refraining from any public offering of its shares. Stay under that ceiling, don't advertise to the general public, and the fund escapes registration as an investment company. The 100-investor cap is why so many hedge funds feel exclusive and hard to access. They literally can't take everyone, so they gravitate toward a smaller number of large investors rather than a crowd of small ones. A modest exception exists for certain small venture capital funds, which can go up to 250 investors under a later law, but the 100-investor rule is the one that shapes most of the industry.

The second exemption is **Section 3(c)(7)**, and it trades one restriction for another. A 3(c)(7) fund faces no cap of 100 investors, but every single investor has to be a qualified purchaser, that five-million-dollar tier from the previous section. The bargain is straightforward: accept only the seriously wealthy and you can accept far more of them. In practice, funds using this exemption still keep their investor count below 2,000, because a separate securities law forces public registration once a fund crosses that threshold, which would defeat the entire purpose of staying private. So 3(c)(7) funds tend to be the larger, more institutional operations, filled with pension funds, endowments, and very wealthy families.

Here's how the two exemptions compare on the terms that determine which one a fund chooses.

Feature	Section 3(c)(1)	Section 3(c)(7)
Investor limit	100 investors	Effectively up to ~2,000
Investor requirement	Accredited investors (in practice)	Qualified purchasers only
Typical fund size	Smaller, emerging managers	Larger, institutional funds
Public offering allowed	No	No

Escaping the Investment Company Act is only half the regulatory picture. The people who run hedge funds also have to reckon with a second law, the **Investment Advisers Act of 1940**, which governs the managers themselves rather than the funds. For decades, a loophole let most hedge fund managers avoid registering as investment advisers with the SEC. Then the 2008 crisis hit, and in its wake Congress passed the Dodd-Frank Act of 2010, which closed the loophole. Now most hedge fund managers overseeing more than 150 million dollars must register with the SEC, submit to periodic examinations, and file disclosures about their operations. This didn't turn hedge funds into mutual funds, not remotely, but it pulled the industry meaningfully further into regulatory daylight than it had ever been before.

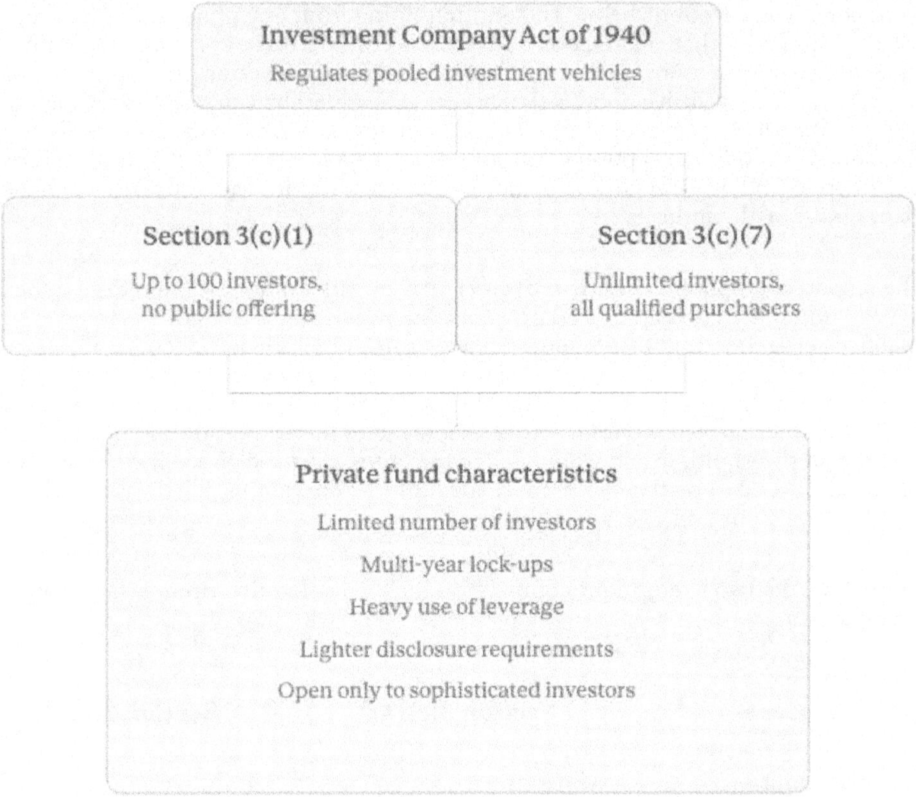

One more piece completes the framework: how these funds are legally allowed to raise money in the first place without running afoul of the rules against selling securities to the public. The answer is **Regulation D**, a set of rules that create safe harbors for private offerings. The provision most hedge funds use, Rule 506(b), lets a fund raise unlimited money from accredited investors without registering the offering publicly, on the condition that the fund doesn't engage in general advertising or solicitation.

This is why, for most of their history, hedge funds operated so quietly. They were legally forbidden from advertising, so they built their businesses through private networks and word of mouth. A newer variant, Rule 506(c), does permit general advertising, but only if the fund restricts itself entirely to accredited investors and takes extra steps to verify each one's status. Most established funds have stuck with the quieter traditional route, which is part of why the industry still carries an air of secrecy even in an age when almost everything else is marketed openly.

Step back and the logic of the whole structure snaps into focus. The wealth requirements, the lock-ups, the redemption gates, the silence about holdings, the exclusivity, none of it is arbitrary. Each feature flows from a deliberate trade the funds have made: give up the public market's broad access and light-touch marketing in return for freedom from the 1940 Act's tight constraints. A hedge fund accepts a small number of wealthy investors, locks up their money, and reveals little, precisely so it can borrow, short, and trade in ways a mutual fund never could. Once you see the trade, every strange feature of the industry becomes readable, and you're ready to look closely at what these funds actually do with the freedom they've bought.

Discussion Question

The accredited investor rules assume that wealth is a reliable proxy for the sophistication needed to evaluate risky, complex investments. Is that assumption defensible? If you were redesigning the system from scratch, what would you use to decide who gets access to these markets, and what would your approach get wrong that the current one gets right?

Chapter 2: The Hedge Fund Business Model

A hedge fund managing 10 billion dollars collects 200 million dollars in fees every year before it earns a single cent for its investors. That's what a 2 percent management fee produces at that size, and it arrives whether the fund goes up, goes down, or does nothing at all. Understand that one number and you understand why so many of the smartest people in finance want to run a hedge fund rather than work at one. The business model is extraordinarily lucrative for the people operating it, and the terms that make it so are the subject of this chapter.

None of this is hidden. The fee structures, the profit splits, the legal skeleton, the choice of where to base the fund, all of it is spelled out in documents every investor signs. But the documents are dense, and the mechanics have real consequences for how much money actually reaches you after the manager takes a cut. So let's take the model apart piece by piece and see how the money moves, who gets it, and why the whole apparatus is built the way it is.

Management Fees and the 2-and-20 Structure

The phrase "2 and 20" is the most famous shorthand in the hedge fund business, and it describes a fee arrangement with two separate parts. The "2" is the management fee: 2 percent of the money you've invested, charged every year, no matter how the fund performs. The "20" is the performance fee, sometimes called the incentive fee or carried interest: 20 percent of any profits the fund generates. Put them together and the deal is this. You pay 2 percent a year just for the privilege of being in the fund, and you hand over one-fifth of whatever gains the manager produces on top of that.

Start with the management fee, because it's the part that surprises people most once they think it through. It's charged on the total assets you've committed, not on profits. That means the manager earns it in good years and bad. If you invest one million dollars and the fund loses 10 percent, you're down to 900,000 dollars and you still owe roughly 20,000 dollars in management fees for the year. The manager made money on your account while you lost it. Defenders explain the fee as covering the cost of running the operation, the salaries, the research, the office, the technology, the compliance staff. That's a fair description of what small funds use it for. At large funds, it's something else entirely.

Consider the arithmetic at scale. A fund with 10 billion dollars under management collects 200 million dollars annually from the management fee alone. No fund needs anywhere near 200 million dollars to pay its analysts and keep the lights on. At that size, the management fee stops being an expense reimbursement and becomes an enormous, guaranteed profit stream that flows to the fund's owners regardless of results. This is the quiet truth of the industry: the biggest managers get spectacularly wealthy from the management fee by itself, entirely apart from whether they're any good at investing. Their performance determines how rich they become, but their survival and comfort are locked in the moment the assets arrive.

Now the performance fee, which is the part that at least aligns the manager's interests with yours. The manager keeps 20 percent of the profits, so the more money she makes for you, the more she makes for herself. If your million-dollar investment grows by 200,000 dollars in a year, the manager takes 20 percent of that gain, or 40,000 dollars, and you keep the remaining 160,000. This is the fee that's supposed to motivate excellence. It only pays out when the fund wins, so in theory the manager is rowing in the same direction as her investors.

Here's a worked example that shows both fees biting at once, using round numbers to keep it clear.

Item	Amount
Your investment	$1,000,000
Fund's gross return for the year	15%, or $150,000 gain
Management fee (2%)	$20,000
Performance fee (20% of $150,000)	$30,000
Total fees paid	$50,000
Your net gain after fees	$100,000
Your effective return	10%

Look at what happened there. The fund earned 15 percent, but you kept 10. Fully a third of your gain went to the manager. In a strong year that split feels tolerable because you still walked away with a healthy return. In a mediocre year it stings badly, and in a losing year you pay the 2 percent management fee for the pain of losing money. Over many years, fees of this magnitude compound into a staggering transfer of wealth from investors to managers. This is the core of the criticism leveled at the industry, and it's a fair one.

The obvious question is why investors ever agreed to terms this steep, and the answer is historical. When hedge funds were young and rare, a handful of managers delivered returns so far above what anyone else could achieve that paying 2 and 20 still left investors far richer than any alternative. If a manager reliably earned 30 percent a year, giving up a third of it was a bargain. The fee structure was priced for genuine scarcity and exceptional skill, and back then that pricing made sense.

The problem is that the fee structure outlived the scarcity. As thousands of hedge funds launched and the industry swelled, the average fund stopped delivering those spectacular returns. Skill got competed away as more smart people crowded into the same trades. Yet the 2 and 20 convention persisted for years even as performance faded, which meant investors were increasingly paying premium prices for ordinary results. That gap between the fees and the value is what drove the backlash of the 2010s and forced the terms to start moving.

And they have moved. The rigid 2 and 20 has softened across most of the industry. Today the averages sit closer to a management fee around 1.4 percent and a performance fee near 16 percent, with plenty of variation. Newer and smaller funds trying to attract capital often cut fees aggressively to compete. Large investors negotiate discounts for writing big checks or agreeing to longer lock-ups. The old numbers survive as a reference point and a symbol, but the actual market has grown more flexible than the famous phrase suggests.

But fees still track genuine, rare skill. When a manager can actually deliver what no one else can, they can name their price. When they can't, competition eventually drags their fees toward the market. The 2 and 20 model isn't really a fixed rule. It's a pricing convention that bends to supply, demand, and demonstrated ability, and the whole recent history of the industry is the story of that convention finally bending.

High-Water Marks and Hurdle Rates

The performance fee, left unchecked, contains a flaw that would let managers charge investors twice for the same gains. Two mechanisms exist to close that flaw, and understanding them separates investors who read their fund documents from those who just sign them.

Picture the problem first. Suppose you invest one million dollars, and in year one the fund earns 20 percent, taking your account to 1.2 million. The manager collects her 20 percent performance fee on that 200,000-dollar gain. Fine, she earned it. Now year two arrives and the fund loses 20 percent, dropping your account back down close to where it started. You've made almost nothing across the two years. Then year three comes and the fund earns that same ground back, climbing again toward 1.2 million. Without any protection, the manager would charge a full performance fee on this third-year recovery, even though she's only clawing back losses from year two. You'd be paying a second performance fee just to return to a value you already reached and already paid fees on. That's obviously unfair, and the high-water mark exists to prevent it.

A **high-water mark** is the highest value your account has ever previously reached, measured at the points where performance fees were charged. The rule is simple and strict: the manager can only collect a performance fee on gains that push your account above its previous high-water mark. Any recovery of prior losses is free. Using the numbers above, after year one your high-water mark is 1.2 million. When the fund falls and then recovers back to 1.2 million, the manager earns nothing on that recovery, because you're only returning to a peak you'd already hit. She starts earning performance fees again only once your account climbs past 1.2 million into genuinely new territory. The high-water mark guarantees you never pay twice for the same dollar of gain.

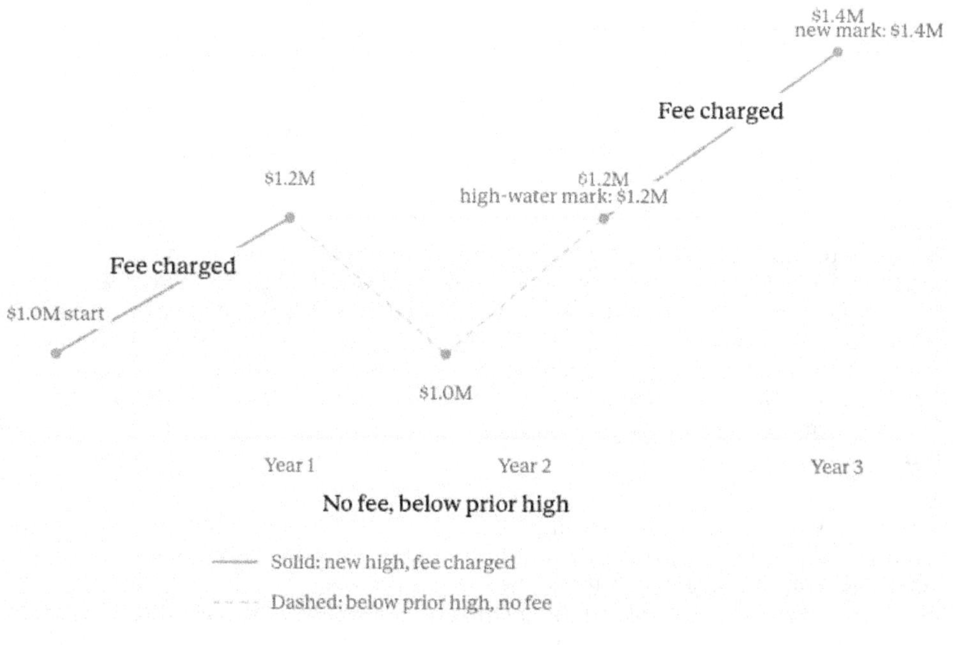

This protection has a sharp consequence for managers, and it's worth appreciating. A manager who suffers a bad year has to earn back all the losses before she sees another dime of performance fees. If a fund drops 40 percent, the manager might have to work for a year or two, generating real returns for investors, while collecting only the management fee and no performance fee at all. For a fund with a lot of employees expecting big bonuses tied to performance fees, a deep loss can be financially devastating to the firm itself. This is why a truly terrible year sometimes kills a hedge fund outright. The manager, staring at a high-water mark far above the current value and realizing it could take years to climb back into performance-fee territory, simply shuts the fund down, returns what's left to investors, and opens a brand-new fund with a fresh high-water mark set at the new starting point. That maneuver, closing a wounded fund to escape an underwater high-water mark and reopening clean, is one of the uglier moves in the business, and it's a reason to pay close attention to a manager's history of fund closures.

The second mechanism is the **hurdle rate**, and it addresses a different objection. Investors reasonably ask why they should pay a performance fee for returns they could've earned with no skill at all. If cash in a safe money-market account pays 5 percent, why should a manager collect a performance fee on the first 5 percent she earns, when a savings account would've delivered that for free? The hurdle rate answers by setting a minimum return the fund must clear before any performance fee kicks in. Only gains above the hurdle count toward the fee.

Hurdle rates come in two flavors, and the difference between them matters more than it first appears.

Type	How It Works	Effect on Investor
Hard hurdle	Performance fee applies only to returns above the hurdle	More favorable, manager earns nothing on the hurdle portion
Soft hurdle	Once returns exceed the hurdle, the fee applies to all gains from zero	Less favorable, the hurdle is just a trigger, not an exclusion

With a hard hurdle set at 5 percent, a fund that returns 12 percent pays a performance fee only on the 7 percentage points above the hurdle. With a soft hurdle at the same 5 percent, once the fund clears 5 percent it charges the performance fee on the entire 12 percent gain, as if the hurdle weren't there at all. The soft hurdle is really just a gate that, once passed, disappears. Both are common, and a hurdle described vaguely as "5 percent" tells you nothing until you know which type it is. This is exactly the kind of detail that separates a good deal from a mediocre one, and it lives in the fine print.

Not every fund uses a hurdle rate at all. Many charge performance fees from the first dollar of gain, with no hurdle whatsoever. Whether a fund includes one, and whether it's hard or soft, is a negotiated term that reflects the manager's leverage over investors. A superstar manager in high demand can refuse a hurdle entirely and still fill the fund. A newer manager hungry for capital might offer a generous hard hurdle to win commitments. Reading these terms tells you something real about the balance of power between a manager and the people funding her.

General Partner and Limited Partner Roles

Underneath the fees sits a legal structure, and it explains who holds power in a hedge fund, who bears risk, and who actually collects all that money. Nearly every hedge fund is organized as a limited partnership, a specific legal form with two distinct kinds of participants whose roles couldn't be more different.

The **limited partners**, or LPs, are the investors. They supply the capital and almost nothing else. They have no say in how the fund invests, no vote on individual trades, no operational role whatsoever. In exchange for that passivity, they get the protection the structure is named for: their liability is limited strictly to the money they put in. If the fund somehow lost more than its assets or got sued into oblivion, an LP could lose the full amount invested but not a dollar more. Their homes, their other assets, their personal wealth beyond the investment stay untouchable. This limited liability is precisely what makes passive investors comfortable handing money to a manager they don't control.

The **general partner**, or GP, sits on the other side. The GP is the entity that runs everything: makes every investment decision, executes the strategy, manages the operation, and carries the legal responsibility for the fund. Traditionally, a general partner in a partnership faces unlimited liability, meaning the GP is on the hook for the fund's obligations beyond just its invested capital. Because unlimited personal liability is a frightening thing to accept, the GP is almost never an individual. Instead it's a limited liability company or a corporation, a separate legal entity that absorbs the liability so the actual humans running the fund don't have to expose their personal wealth. The manager sets up a company to be the GP, and that company shoulders the legal risk.

There's a further wrinkle that confuses newcomers, and it's worth untangling because it explains how the money is really split. In most hedge fund setups, the fees don't all flow to a single entity. The arrangement typically separates into two:

The **management company** is the operating business. It employs the analysts, the traders, the back-office staff. It receives the management fee, the 2 percent, and uses that money to pay salaries and cover the cost of running the firm.

The **general partner entity** is a separate vehicle that receives the performance fee, the 20 percent share of profits, which in this structure is often called the performance allocation rather than a fee. It's carved out separately for tax reasons, because profits routed this way can qualify for more favorable tax treatment than ordinary fee income.

This split between the management company and the GP entity is why the same manager might control several related legal entities that all serve different functions. The person you think of as "the hedge fund manager" typically owns both the management company collecting the flat fee and the GP entity collecting the profit share, so all the money ends up in the same hands, just through two channels arranged for tax efficiency and liability protection.

That tax angle deserves a note, because it's one of the most contested features of the entire industry. The performance allocation the GP receives is frequently treated as a capital gain rather than as ordinary income, and capital gains are taxed at meaningfully lower rates than the wages the rest of us earn. This is the famous carried interest treatment, and it means a hedge fund manager can pay a lower tax rate on hundreds of millions of dollars in profit share than a salaried employee pays on a normal paycheck. Politicians have attacked the carried interest treatment for years and repeatedly promised to close it, and it has proven remarkably durable, surviving reform after reform. Whatever you think of its fairness, it's a real and large part of why running the GP side of a hedge fund is so financially attractive.

Fund Domicile: Onshore vs. Offshore Structures

Ask where a hedge fund is "located" and you'll often get two answers, because most funds of any size exist in two places at once. A single strategy frequently runs through parallel structures, one based in the United States and another registered somewhere like the Cayman Islands. This isn't secrecy for its own sake or an attempt to hide from regulators. It's a response to the fact that different investors face wildly different tax situations, and no single structure serves all of them well.

The **onshore** fund is the domestic vehicle, typically organized as a Delaware limited partnership. Delaware dominates because its laws around business entities are well-developed, predictable, and favorable, so the legal ground is solid and familiar to every lawyer in the field. The onshore fund is built for United States investors who pay taxes, ordinary taxable Americans, wealthy individuals and families, who want to invest in the fund. For them, the limited partnership structure works cleanly, because partnerships pass their income straight through to the investors, who then report it on their own tax returns. There's no separate layer of tax at the fund level, which is exactly what a taxable US investor wants.

The **offshore** fund is the foreign vehicle, most commonly registered in the Cayman Islands, though Bermuda and the British Virgin Islands also see heavy use. Unlike the onshore partnership, the offshore fund is usually structured as a corporation. It exists to serve two groups the onshore fund can't serve well: investors who aren't United States taxpayers, and, importantly, United States tax-exempt investors like pension funds, university endowments, and charitable foundations.

That second group is the part that puzzles people. Why would a tax-exempt American institution, one that pays no taxes anyway, need a foreign fund? The answer is a technical tax problem with a plain-language cause. When a tax-exempt organization invests in a partnership that borrows money to invest, the profits attributable to that borrowing can become taxable to the organization under a rule targeting what's called unrelated business taxable income. A charity that pays no tax on its normal activities can suddenly owe tax on hedge fund gains simply because the fund used borrowing. Routing the investment through an offshore corporation solves the problem. The corporate structure absorbs the issue and prevents that taxable income from flowing through to the tax-exempt investor, letting the endowment or pension fund keep its tax-free status intact. The offshore fund isn't about hiding money. For these investors, it's about not triggering a tax they'd otherwise be forced to pay.

The Cayman Islands earned its dominant position for practical reasons rather than sinister ones. It imposes no additional layer of tax at the fund level, so money passing through isn't taxed twice. Its regulatory system is built specifically to accommodate investment funds efficiently. And it offers legal stability and a deep bench of professionals, lawyers, administrators, auditors, who specialize in exactly this work. The reputation of offshore centers as havens for illicit money has attached some stigma to the arrangement, but the mainstream use by pension funds and endowments is thoroughly legal and openly disclosed to regulators.

Running two separate funds for the same strategy would be a headache if the manager had to make every trade twice, once in each fund. The industry solved this with an elegant arrangement called the **master-feeder structure**, which has become the standard for funds serving both domestic and foreign investors.

Here's how it fits together. The two funds investors actually put money into, the onshore partnership and the offshore corporation, are called feeder funds. Neither one trades directly. Instead, both feed all their capital into a single central entity called the master fund, and the master fund is where all the actual investing happens. The manager trades one book, inside the master fund, and the profits and losses flow back proportionally to the two feeders and then out to their respective investors. Everyone gets the same investment results because everyone's money is pooled in the same master, but each type of investor enters through the feeder built for their particular tax situation.

Structure	Legal Form	Serves	Purpose
Onshore feeder	Delaware limited partnership	US taxable investors	Pass-through income, no fund-level tax
Offshore feeder	Cayman corporation	Non-US and US tax-exempt investors	Avoids adverse tax on tax-exempts, serves foreign investors
Master fund	Usually offshore	Both feeders pooled together	Single place where all trading occurs

The beauty of this design is efficiency. The manager makes decisions once, executes once, and maintains one portfolio, while the branching structure above it quietly sorts each investor into the right tax treatment without anyone experiencing different investment performance. It looks complicated on a diagram, and the underlying logic is simple: pool the trading in one place, split the entrances by tax status. Once you

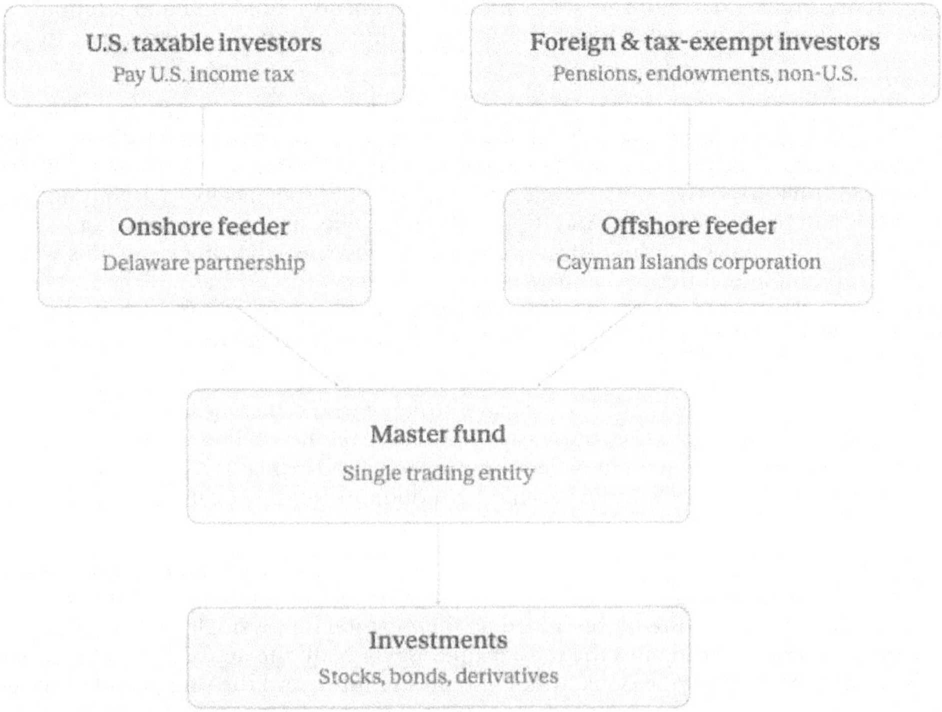

see that, the master-feeder structure stops looking like a scheme and starts looking like what it is – a sensible answer to the problem of serving investors who live under very different tax rules but want access to the same manager.

Discussion Question

The management fee pays a manager handsomely whether investors win or lose, while the performance fee only pays when they win. If you were structuring a fund from scratch and wanted the manager's incentives to line up as closely as possible with your own, how would you weight these two fees against each other, and what would go wrong if you pushed too far in either direction?

Chapter 3: Long/Short Equity Strategies

Ordinary investors have exactly one way to make money: buy something and hope it goes up. If they're convinced a company is rotten, the best they can do is refuse to own it. A long/short manager has a second option, and it changes everything. She can bet against the rotten company and profit when it falls. That one addition, the ability to make money when a stock drops, doubles the ways a manager can be right, and it defines the oldest hedge fund strategy there is.

Long/short equity is where the entire industry began, back when Alfred Winslow Jones combined owned stocks with bet-against stocks and borrowed money to size up both. Decades later it remains the largest single category of hedge funds, home to some of the most famous names in finance. The strategy sounds simple when you state it: buy the good ones, short the bad ones.

Doing it well is brutally hard, and the mechanics underneath it are richer than the one-line summary suggests. This chapter takes apart how managers pick their bets, how they neutralize the market's influence when they want to, why the plumbing of short selling matters so much, and how the most aggressive practitioners don't just bet on companies but try to change them.

Fundamental Stock Selection and Alpha Generation

To understand what a long/short manager is really chasing, you have to separate two sources of return that get tangled together in every stock you own.

When a stock you hold rises 10 percent, part of that gain usually has nothing to do with the specific company. If the entire market went up 8 percent that week, most stocks rode the wave, and your stock's rise was mostly just the tide lifting everything. Only the portion of the return that came from something particular to that company, its earnings surprise, a new product, a smart acquisition, represents genuine stock-picking skill. Finance has names for these two pieces. **Beta** is the part of a stock's return that comes from moving with the overall market. **Alpha** is the part that comes from something specific to that stock, the piece a skilled manager can actually claim credit for.

This distinction sits at the center of the whole enterprise. Anyone can capture beta. You get it for almost nothing by buying an index fund that rises and falls with the market. Nobody should pay a hedge fund manager 20 percent of profits for beta, because beta is free. What justifies the fees, if anything does, is alpha: the return a manager generates through insight that the market's general direction doesn't explain. Long/short equity, at its purest, is an attempt to strip away beta and deliver alpha on its own. A manager who owns good stocks and shorts bad ones in roughly equal measure has arranged her book so that the market's up-and-down movement largely cancels out, leaving the difference in performance between her longs and her shorts. That difference is her alpha, laid bare.

Total return = beta + alpha

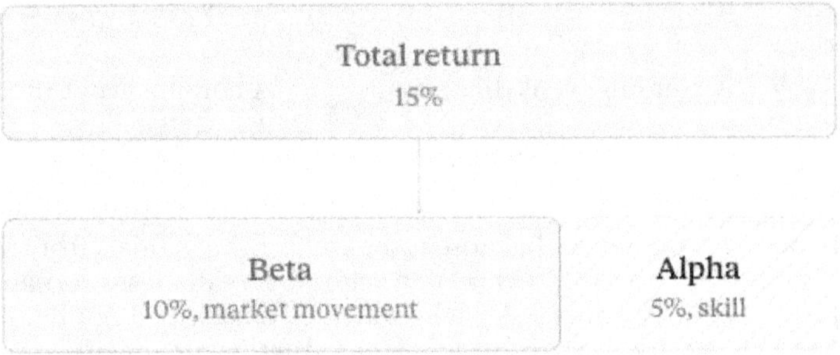

Generating it starts with fundamental analysis, which is the patient work of figuring out what a company is actually worth and comparing that to what the market is charging for it. A fundamental analyst reads financial statements line by line, studies the industry, interviews customers and former employees, builds models of future cash flows, and forms a judgment about whether a stock is cheap, expensive, or fairly priced. The long side of the book comes from finding businesses trading below what they're worth, companies with durable advantages, competent management, strong balance sheets, and a price that doesn't reflect their prospects.

The short side is where the real craft shows, because shorting well is far harder than buying well. A good short candidate isn't merely a mediocre company. Mediocre companies can drift along for years, even decades, without falling. A compelling short usually has something actively wrong with it that the market hasn't fully recognized: fading demand for its core product, a balance sheet buckling under debt, accounting that doesn't add up, a business model being quietly destroyed by a competitor, or outright fraud. The short seller's job is to spot the deterioration before the crowd does and profit as reality catches up to the stock price.

Here's a rough sketch of what distinguishes a strong long thesis from a strong short thesis, though the best managers weigh dozens of factors beyond these.

Element	Strong Long Candidate	Strong Short Candidate
Valuation	Trading below intrinsic worth	Priced far above any reasonable value
Business trajectory	Growing, gaining market share	Declining, losing ground to rivals
Balance sheet	Low debt, strong cash generation	Heavy debt, burning cash
Management	Capable, honest, aligned with shareholders	Promotional, evasive, or self-dealing

Accounting	Clean, conservative	Aggressive, opaque, hard to verify
Catalyst	A coming event that reveals the value	A coming event that exposes the weakness

That last row deserves emphasis, because it separates professionals from amateurs. Being right that a stock is overvalued isn't enough. Overvalued stocks can stay overvalued for years, and a short seller who's early can be wiped out before being proven correct. What a good short needs is a **catalyst**, some specific event or trend that will force the market to see what the manager already sees: an earnings miss, a debt maturity the company can't refinance, a product recall, a regulatory ruling, an accounting restatement. Without a catalyst, a short thesis is just an opinion about value with no timeline, and in markets, timing is the difference between genius and ruin.

Jim Chanos built a career on exactly this kind of work. Running his firm Kynikos Associates, Chanos specialized in finding companies whose reported success masked underlying rot. His most celebrated call was Enron, which he began shorting in 2000 after studying its financial statements and concluding the company's reported profits didn't correspond to any real cash. He noticed the accounting was designed to obscure rather than reveal, and he saw insiders selling stock while telling the public everything was fine. When Enron collapsed into bankruptcy in 2001, Chanos was proven spectacularly right, and the episode became the template for fundamental short selling: read what others skip, trust the numbers over the story, and wait for the catalyst that forces the truth into the open. Chanos has traditionally been 2x long the market through plain indexing while being 1x short the market through individual calls where the intellectual capital of the fund is put to work.

The generation of alpha through this kind of analysis is the intellectual core of long/short investing, and it's worth being sober about how difficult it is. The market is crowded with intelligent, well-resourced people all doing the same research, which means genuine insight, the kind that isn't already reflected in the price, is scarce and getting scarcer. Many managers who believe they're producing alpha are actually just collecting disguised beta and charging alpha prices for it. Distinguishing real skill from luck (i.e., positive variance) or hidden market exposure takes years of data and careful analysis, which is a problem this book returns to when it examines how investors evaluate managers. For now, hold onto the central idea: the entire justification for a long/short manager's existence rests on her ability to produce returns that the market's movement can't explain.

Pair Trading and Market Neutrality

The cleanest way to strip beta out of a portfolio is to build it in matched pairs, and the technique that does this is one of the most elegant ideas in trading.

Pair trading starts with two companies so similar that they normally move in tandem. Think of two large beverage makers, or two big automakers, or two competing retailers in the same segment. Because they face the same industry conditions, the same economic winds, the same customer trends, their stock prices tend to rise and fall together. The pairs trader watches the relationship between them and waits for it to stretch abnormally, for one stock to run ahead of its partner in a way that history suggests won't last. When that gap widens beyond its normal range, the trader shorts the one that's gotten expensive and buys the one that's lagged, betting that the two will converge back toward their usual relationship.

Notice what this accomplishes. The trader isn't betting on the beverage industry going up or down. She's long one beverage company and short another, so whatever happens to the sector as a whole washes out. If a sugar tax tanks both stocks, she loses on her long and gains on her short, roughly canceling. Her profit comes entirely from the gap between the two closing, from the relative performance of the pair, not from any market direction. This is beta stripped away almost completely, leaving something close to pure relative judgment.

The strategy has real intellectual pedigree. It grew out of the quantitative trading groups at Morgan Stanley in the 1980s, where a team including Gerry Bamberger developed early systematic pairs trading, later refined by the firm's statistical arbitrage desk. The core insight, that you can profit from the relationship between two securities while remaining indifferent to the market itself, opened the door to an entire family of market-neutral strategies.

A **market-neutral** fund extends the pair-trading logic across an entire portfolio. Rather than a handful of matched pairs, the manager assembles a large book of longs and a large book of shorts, balanced so that the portfolio's overall sensitivity to the market, its net beta, sits near zero. Constructed properly, such a fund should make money in a rising market, a falling market, or a flat one, because its returns come from the longs outperforming the shorts, not from the direction of stocks in general. This is the closest the industry gets to the pure absolute return ideal, a return stream genuinely disconnected from what the broader market does.

Now comes a point that reshapes how you should think about the entire value of hedge funds, and it's worth slowing down for.

Investors instinctively judge a fund by one question: did it beat the market? That's the wrong question for a strategy like this, and understanding why is one of the more important ideas in the whole field. Part of the value a hedge fund delivers has nothing to do with beating the market. It comes from **producing a return stream that behaves differently from the market**, one with low, zero, or even negative correlation to common benchmarks. A fund that earns a steady 6 percent while barely moving in relation to the S&P 500 might look unimpressive next to an index that returned 10 percent last year. But that comparison misses what the fund is actually for.

Consider what happens when you combine two return streams. If you own a portfolio of stocks and add an investment that moves in perfect lockstep with those stocks, you haven't reduced your risk at all. You've just made a bigger version of the same bet. But if you add an investment whose returns are uncorrelated with your stocks, something remarkable happens to the combination. The ups and downs partially offset each other, and the blended portfolio becomes steadier than either piece alone. Your overall risk falls without a matching fall in return. And if you add an investment that's negatively correlated, one that tends to rise when your stocks fall, it behaves like insurance, cushioning your worst moments precisely when you need it most.

Here's a simplified illustration of the effect, comparing what happens when you blend a stock portfolio with two different additions.

Scenario	Stock Portfolio Alone	Blended with Correlated Asset	Blended with Uncorrelated Asset
Expected return	8%	8%	7%
Volatility (risk)	High	Still high	Meaningfully lower
Behavior in a crash	Falls hard	Falls hard	Falls less, cushioned
Return per unit of risk	Moderate	Moderate	Higher

Look at the rightmost column. The uncorrelated asset returned slightly less on its own, 7 percent instead of 8, yet the blended portfolio delivers more return for each unit of risk taken. This is the counterintuitive heart of it. An investment that earns less than the market can still improve your overall results, because what it contributes isn't just return, it's a different pattern of returns that offsets the swings in what you already own. And a fund that scaled back to the same risk through prudent leverage or leverage-like techniques could actually outperform. The measure investors use for return-per-unit-of-risk is called the Sharpe ratio, and a decorrelated return stream can lift a whole portfolio's Sharpe ratio even when its standalone return trails the market.

This reframes the entire pitch of market-neutral and low-correlation hedge funds. They aren't promising to beat the S&P 500 in a good year, and they'll usually lose that contest during a bull market. What they're offering is a return that shows up regardless of what stocks do, a source of gains that doesn't rise and fall with the rest of your holdings. For an investor who already owns plenty of stocks, and most large investors are stuffed with stock market exposure, the last thing they need is more of the same risk. They need something that behaves independently. A modest return that arrives on its own schedule, unbothered by market crashes, can be worth more to such an investor than a higher return that simply amplifies the risk they're already drowning in.

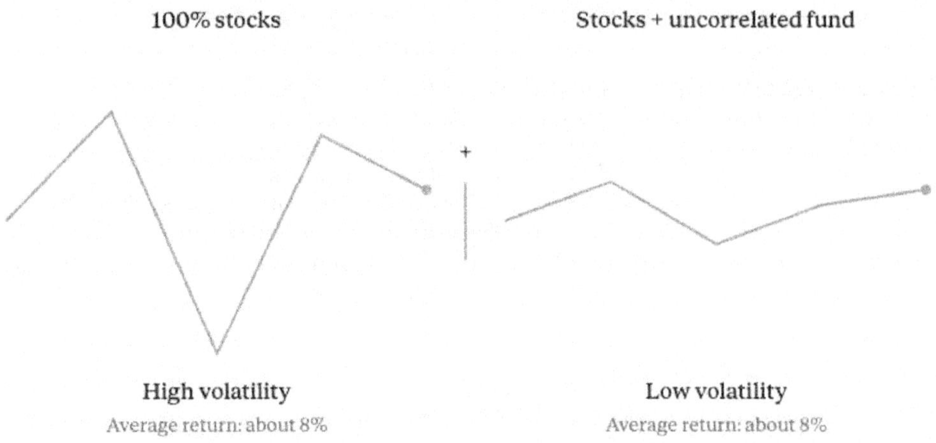

This is why sophisticated institutions pay for these strategies even when the raw returns look ordinary. A pension fund isn't buying a lottery ticket on the next bull market. It's assembling a collection of return streams that behave differently from one another, so that no single bad event can sink the whole portfolio. A market-neutral fund earning a steady, uncorrelated return is a genuinely useful component of that collection, in a way that a high-flying but market-correlated fund isn't. The value isn't in the size of the return. It's in the independence of the return.

The catch, and there's always a catch, is that true market neutrality is harder to maintain than it looks. Correlations that hold in calm markets can break down in crises, when everything moves together and the careful offsetting relationships a manager relied upon suddenly stop working. A fund that appears market-neutral for years can discover, in a panic, that its longs and shorts have started falling in unison. The decorrelation is real but conditional, and the funds that survive are the ones that never mistake a calm-weather relationship for an ironclad law.

Gross Exposure vs. Net Exposure

To read a long/short fund's actual risk, you need two numbers, and confusing them is one of the most common mistakes newcomers make.

Imagine a fund with 100 million dollars in capital. It uses that capital to buy 100 million dollars of stocks it likes and, separately, to short 80 million dollars of stocks it dislikes. Two very different measurements describe what this fund is doing, and each tells you something the other hides.

Net exposure measures the fund's directional bet on the market. You calculate it by subtracting the shorts from the longs: 100 million long minus 80 million short leaves

20 million of net long exposure, or 20 percent of the fund's capital. This number tells you how much the fund will move with the market. A net exposure of 20 percent means the fund is only lightly tied to market direction. If the market rises, this fund participates a little, but not much, because most of its long bet is offset by its short bet. Net exposure is the beta measurement, the answer to "how much does this fund ride the market's waves?"

Gross exposure measures the total size of the fund's positions, ignoring which direction they point. You calculate it by adding the longs and shorts together: 100 million long plus 80 million short equals 180 million of gross exposure, or 180 percent of the fund's capital. This number tells you how much the fund is actually doing, how much borrowing it's using, and how much risk it's carrying from its individual stock picks. A fund with 180 percent gross exposure has put far more money at work than the capital it holds, which it accomplishes through borrowing. Gross exposure is the measurement of total activity and the borrowing behind it.

The two numbers can tell wildly different stories about the same fund, which is exactly why you need both. Here are several funds, each holding 100 million dollars of capital, arranged so different profiles become visible.

Fund Profile	Long	Short	Net Exposure	Gross Exposure	What It Means
Traditional long-only	$100M	$0	100%	100%	Fully exposed to market direction, no borrowing
Modestly hedged	$100M	$40M	60%	140%	Leans bullish, some downside protection
Market neutral	$100M	$100M	0%	200%	No market bet, high total activity
Aggressive 130/30	$130M	$30M	100%	160%	Full market bet plus extra stock selection
Net short (bearish)	$60M	$100M	-40%	160%	Betting the market falls

Study the market-neutral row. Its net exposure is zero, meaning it makes no directional bet on the market whatsoever, exactly the decorrelated profile discussed earlier. But its gross exposure is 200 percent, meaning it has twice its capital deployed in positions. A careless observer looking only at net exposure would call this a low-risk fund, since it isn't betting on market direction. But the 200 percent gross tells you the fund is carrying substantial risk from its individual stock selections, amplified by borrowing. If its longs and shorts move against it, the losses come fast, market-neutral or not. The zero net exposure protects against market moves. It does nothing to protect against the manager simply being wrong about which stocks are good and which are bad.

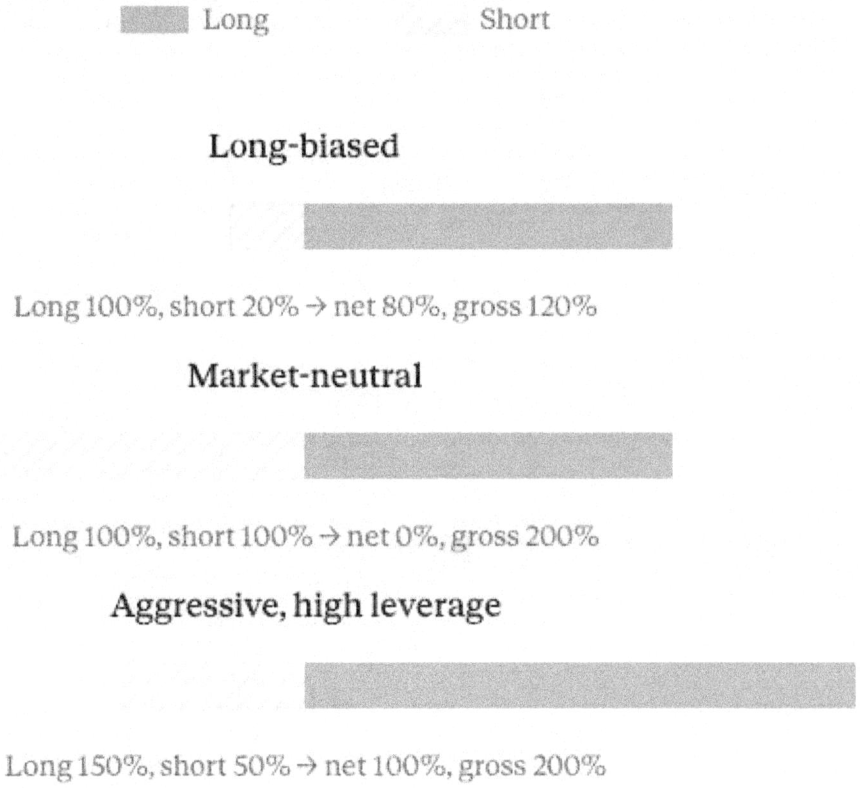

This is the practical lesson. Net exposure tells you the fund's vulnerability to the market. Gross exposure tells you the fund's vulnerability to its own convictions and how much borrowing magnifies them. A fund can be market-neutral and still enormously risky if its gross exposure is high, because it's making large, borrowed bets on individual stocks even while hedging out the market. When you evaluate any long/short fund, both numbers belong in front of you, because either one alone paints a misleading picture.

Short Selling Mechanics and Borrow Costs

Everything about long/short investing depends on the ability to short, and short selling is stranger and more fragile than most people realize. Buying a stock is intuitive: you pay money, you own a thing, you can hold it forever if you like. Shorting inverts all of that, and the inversion creates risks that have destroyed even brilliant investors.

Here's the mechanical sequence. To short a stock, you first borrow shares you don't own, usually from a broker who sources them from other clients' holdings. You immediately sell those borrowed shares on the open market and collect the cash. Later, you buy the same number of shares back, hopefully at a lower price, and return them to the lender. This final step is called covering. Your profit is the difference between the price you sold at and the lower price you bought back at. If the stock fell from 50 dollars to 30, you sold borrowed shares at 50, bought them back at 30, returned them, and pocketed 20 dollars per share. You made money on a stock going down, which is the entire point.

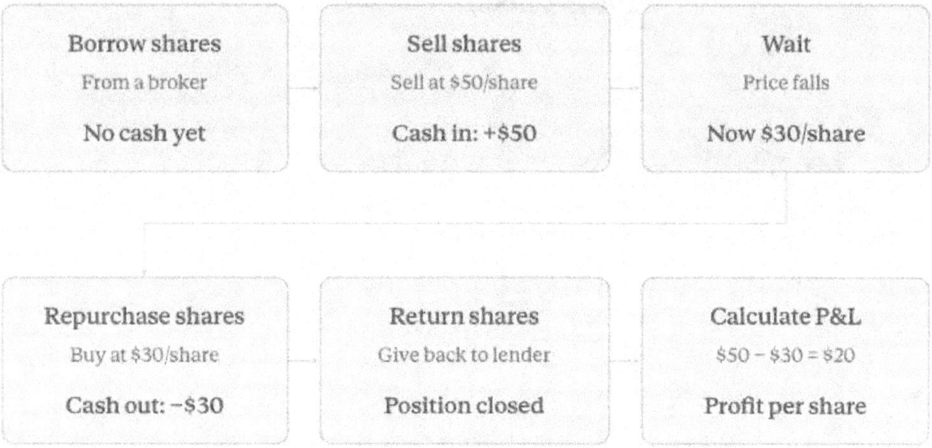

Cash flows in at the sale, out at the repurchase

Borrowing shares isn't free, and the cost is a real drag on every short position. The lender charges a fee for lending the stock, quoted as an annualized rate called the borrow cost or borrow fee. For a stock that's easy to borrow, plentiful and widely held, this fee is tiny, sometimes a fraction of a percent per year. For a stock that's hard to borrow, one where shares are scarce and many people want to short it, the fee can climb to double digits annually, occasionally far higher. A stock costing 30 percent a year to borrow means your short is losing 30 percent annually to fees alone before the stock moves at all. These hard-to-borrow situations often arise precisely around the most attractive short targets, the troubled companies everyone suspects, which creates a cruel dynamic: the shorts you most want to put on are frequently the most expensive to hold.

Now the risk that makes shorting genuinely dangerous, and it's a matter of simple arithmetic. When you buy a stock, the worst that can happen is it goes to zero, and you lose 100 percent of what you invested. Your loss is capped, and your potential gain is unlimited, since a stock can rise forever. Shorting reverses this asymmetry completely, and the reversal is punishing.

Position	Maximum Loss	Maximum Gain

Buying (long)	100%, if the stock goes to zero	Unlimited, the stock can rise forever
Shorting	Unlimited, the stock can rise forever	Capped at 100%, the stock can only fall to zero

Read the short row carefully. Your maximum gain on a short is 100 percent, achieved only if the stock goes all the way to zero. But your maximum loss is unlimited, because the stock you're short can rise without limit, and every dollar it rises is a dollar you lose. Short a stock at 50 dollars and watch it climb to 200, and you've lost 150 dollars per share on a position that could've only ever made you 50. The math is stacked against you in a way it never is when buying. This asymmetry means short sellers must manage their positions with far more discipline than long investors, because a single short that runs against them can inflict losses larger than the entire position was ever worth.

That danger becomes catastrophic in an event called a **short squeeze**, which is the short seller's nightmare made real. When a heavily shorted stock starts rising, the short sellers begin losing money, and some are forced to cover, meaning they buy shares back to close their positions and stop the bleeding. But their buying pushes the stock even higher, which inflicts more losses on the remaining shorts, which forces more of them to cover, which drives the price higher still. The feedback loop feeds on itself, and a stock can rocket to absurd heights not because anything improved at the company but purely because trapped short sellers are scrambling to buy their way out.

The GameStop episode of January 2021 turned a short squeeze into a global spectacle. GameStop, a declining video game retailer, was heavily shorted by hedge funds who reasonably believed the business was dying. A crowd of individual investors, coordinating on the internet, recognized the enormous short interest and began buying the stock deliberately to trigger a squeeze. It worked beyond anyone's imagination. The stock rose from a few dollars to hundreds within weeks, and the hedge funds short the stock suffered staggering losses. Melvin Capital, one of the most prominent shorts, lost billions of dollars and required a cash injection from other funds to survive the month. It never fully recovered and shut down the following year. The episode was a vivid, public lesson in the unlimited-loss nature of shorting, and a reminder that being right about a company's fundamentals offers no protection against a squeeze in the short run.

An older example shows the same force at even greater extremes. In 2008, Volkswagen briefly became the most valuable company in the world, not because of anything it did, but because Porsche had quietly accumulated control of most of its available shares. Short sellers who'd bet against Volkswagen suddenly found there were almost no shares available to buy back, and the resulting scramble sent the stock up several hundred percent in two days before it collapsed again. Fortunes were lost in hours. The lesson threading through both stories is that short selling exposes you to forces that buying never does, and no amount of analytical brilliance about a company's true worth can save you from a squeeze while it's happening.

Activist Investing and Shareholder Campaigns

Most long/short managers take positions and wait for their thesis to play out, passive observers of companies they don't control. Activist investors reject that patience entirely. Rather than betting on what a company will do, they buy a large stake and then try to force the company to do what they want, transforming themselves from spectators into participants in the outcome.

The activist playbook runs like this. The investor quietly accumulates a meaningful position in a company she believes is underperforming its potential, often because of a management team making poor decisions, a bloated cost structure, a misguided strategy, or a corporate structure that hides value. Once she holds enough shares to command attention, she goes public with a demand: sell a division, replace the CEO, return cash to shareholders, cut costs, split the company in two, or put the whole thing up for sale. She makes her case loudly, through letters, presentations, and media appearances, arguing that her changes would lift the stock. If management resists, the fight can escalate into a proxy battle, a campaign to win seats on the company's board of directors by persuading other shareholders to vote with her. The activist's power comes from other investors: if enough of them agree, management has to bend.

The tactics vary widely in tone, from cordial persuasion to open warfare. Some activists work behind the scenes, pressing their case in private meetings and only going public as a last resort. Others weaponize publicity from the start. Dan Loeb, who runs Third Point, became notorious for writing scathing public letters to the executives of companies he targeted, mocking their competence in language designed to embarrass them and rally other shareholders to his side. Carl Icahn, one of the most feared activists of his generation, built a decades-long career on aggressive campaigns that often ended with companies capitulating to his demands rather than endure a prolonged public fight with him.

Here's a sampling of notable activist campaigns and how they turned out, which conveys the range of what these investors attempt and how unpredictable the results can be.

Activist	Target	Demand	Outcome
Nelson Peltz (Trian)	Procter & Gamble, 2017	Board seat, operational overhaul	Won a board seat after one of the largest, closest proxy fights ever
Carl Icahn	Apple, 2013	Larger stock buybacks	Apple expanded buybacks, though on its own terms
Dan Loeb (Third Point)	Yahoo, 2011-2012	CEO removal, board changes	Forced out the CEO, gained board seats, reshaped the company

Bill Ackman (Pershing Square)	Herbalife, 2012-2018	Public short, alleged pyramid scheme	Lost roughly a billion dollars as the stock rose against him

The Herbalife row is a cautionary tale worth dwelling on, because it captures how badly activism can go. Bill Ackman, a prominent activist, took an enormous short position in Herbalife and then launched a public crusade against it, arguing the company was a pyramid scheme that regulators would eventually shut down. He presented hours of research, lobbied government agencies, and staked his reputation on the company's collapse. But another famous investor, Carl Icahn, took the opposite side, buying a large long position partly out of conviction and partly, by many accounts, out of personal animosity toward Ackman. The two clashed publicly, including a legendary live shouting match on financial television. Herbalife never collapsed. The stock rose over the years Ackman held his short, and he eventually exited the position at a loss estimated near a billion dollars. The saga is a reminder that activism, especially activism on the short side, pits your analysis against a living company that fights back, against other investors who may take the other side, and against the possibility that you're simply wrong.

Activist investing also raises a genuine debate about whether it helps or harms the companies involved, and reasonable people land on opposite sides. Defenders argue that activists impose discipline on lazy or entrenched management, unlocking value that benefits all shareholders and forcing underperforming executives to sharpen up or step aside. Critics counter that many activists chase short-term stock gains at the expense of a company's long-term health, pushing for buybacks and cost cuts that juice the share price for a few quarters while hollowing out the business's future. Both critiques describe real cases. Some activist campaigns have rescued failing companies from complacent leadership. Others have loaded healthy companies with debt to fund payouts, then departed with their profits before the damage showed. The truth is that activism is a tool, and like most tools its effect depends entirely on who's wielding it and why.

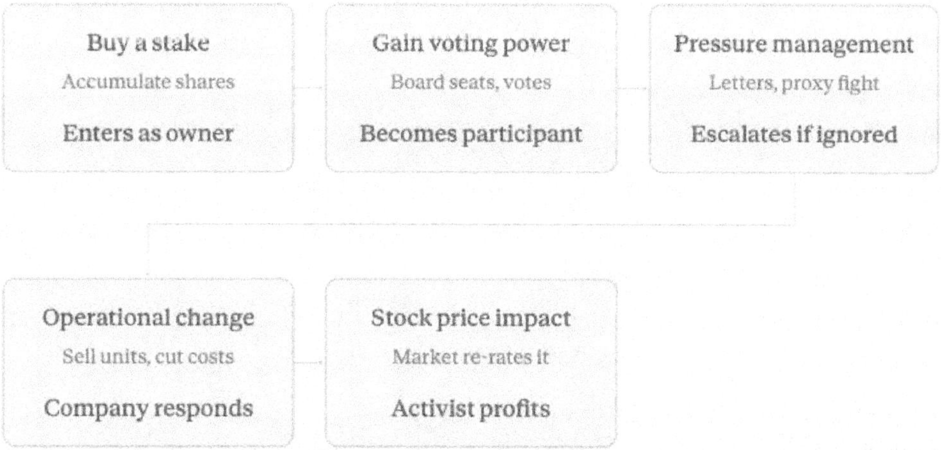

From spectator to participant in the outcome

What unites activist investing with everything else in this chapter is the underlying long/short logic. An activist is usually long the company she's trying to fix, betting that her interventions will lift the stock she owns. Some activists run the strategy in reverse, taking short positions and then publicly exposing what they believe is wrong with a company, profiting as the stock falls in response to their revelations. Firms like Muddy Waters and Hindenburg Research built their reputations this way, publishing detailed reports alleging fraud or deception at companies they'd shorted, then watching the stocks tumble as the market absorbed the accusations. Whether working from the long side or the short side, the activist is doing what every long/short manager does, forming a view about a company's true value, but with one radical addition: instead of waiting for the market to agree, she tries to force the outcome herself.

Discussion Question

A market-neutral fund that returns a steady 6 percent with no correlation to the stock market will lose badly, on paper, to an index fund in any strong bull year, and its investors will be tempted to abandon it for underperforming. Yet its independence from the market is exactly what makes it valuable inside a larger portfolio. How should an investor decide when a decorrelated but lower-returning strategy is genuinely earning its place, versus when "low correlation" has become an excuse for mediocre returns that simply aren't worth the fees?

Chapter 4: Global Macro and Managed Futures

A stock picker spends months studying a single company. A global macro trader can wake up, bet that the Japanese yen will weaken, that Brazilian interest rates will fall, that oil will rise, and that German government bonds will drop, and have all four positions on before lunch. The canvas isn't a company or even an industry. It's the entire global economy, every currency, every bond market, every commodity, every central bank decision, all of it fair game. This breadth is what makes global macro the most freewheeling strategy in the hedge fund business, and it attracts a particular kind of mind: people who want to bet on how the whole system moves rather than on the fate of any one firm.

Global macro and its close relative, managed futures, share a common feature that sets them apart from the stock-picking strategies of the last chapter. They trade the big instruments of the financial system, currencies, government bonds, interest rates, stock indices, and commodities, often through futures contracts or other derivatives, and they form their views from the top down, starting with the largest economic forces and working toward specific trades. Some practitioners rely on human judgment and intuition. Others hand every decision to computer models that follow strict rules.

This chapter walks through how these traders read the economy, how they express their views through currencies and interest rates, how the systematic trend-followers operate, and how the human-driven and machine-driven camps differ in ways that matter to anyone deciding where to put money.

Top-Down Economic Analysis

The defining habit of a macro trader is thinking from the top down, and it's worth understanding exactly what that means, because it inverts the approach of most investors.

A stock picker works from the bottom up. She starts with a specific company, digs into its financials, evaluates its management, and builds a view of that one business, then repeats the process for the next company. The broad economy is background noise she mostly tries to hedge away. A macro trader does the opposite. She starts with the biggest picture imaginable, the direction of the global economy, the policies of central banks, the flow of capital between countries, and works downward toward a trade that expresses her view of those enormous forces. The individual company barely enters the picture. What matters is the system: growth, inflation, interest rates, debt, trade, and politics, and how they push against one another.

The raw material of this analysis is economic data, and a macro trader consumes it constantly. Gross domestic product tells her whether an economy is expanding or contracting. Inflation figures tell her whether prices are rising fast enough to force a central bank's hand. Unemployment numbers reveal the slack or tightness in a labor market. Trade balances show which countries are running surpluses and which are bleeding money abroad. Government budgets, consumer spending, manufacturing surveys, housing starts, and a hundred other indicators all feed into a picture of where each major economy stands and where it's heading. The macro trader's job is to assemble these pieces into a coherent view and then find the imbalance, the place where the current state of things can't persist and something has to give.

That word, imbalance, sits at the heart of macro thinking. Markets and economies are full of relationships that drift out of alignment: a currency propped up above its natural value, interest rates held artificially low, a country borrowing more than it can sustain, an asset priced for a future that isn't coming. The macro trader hunts for these tensions and positions herself for the correction. She's betting that reality will eventually reassert itself, that the overvalued currency will fall, that the unsustainable borrowing will trigger a crisis, that the mispriced asset will snap back. The skill lies in spotting the imbalance before others do and, harder still, in judging when it will finally resolve, because an imbalance can persist far longer than seems possible before it breaks.

Ray Dalio, who built Bridgewater Associates into one of the largest hedge fund firms in the world, made this kind of systematic economic thinking the foundation of his entire operation. Dalio developed a framework he calls the economic machine, a model of how economies function driven by productivity growth over the long run and by cycles of debt over the shorter run. He argued that most economic movements can be understood as the interaction of a few basic forces: how much an economy produces, how much it borrows, and how those debts eventually have to be repaid or restructured. Studying the mechanics of these debt cycles, Bridgewater tried to anticipate major economic shifts before they arrived. The firm's willingness to reduce economics to a set of understandable cause-and-effect relationships, and to build repeatable rules from them, exemplifies the top-down mindset at its most rigorous.

The flexibility of the macro approach is its great advantage. A stock picker is confined to stocks. A macro trader, having formed a view, can choose from an enormous menu of ways to express it, picking whichever instrument offers the cleanest bet with the best odds. Suppose a trader concludes that a country's economy is overheating and its central bank will be forced to raise interest rates. She could act on that single view through several different trades:

View	Possible Trade	Instrument Used
Central bank will raise rates	Bet that the country's bonds fall	Government bond futures
Higher rates will strengthen the currency	Buy the currency	Currency forwards or futures

Rate hikes will slow the economy	Bet the stock market falls	Stock index futures
Rates rising faster than expected	Bet directly on the rate path	Interest rate futures

Notice how one economic view spawns four distinct trades, each with different risks and payoffs. The macro trader's craft includes not just forming the view but choosing the instrument that expresses it most efficiently, the one where she gets paid the most if she's right and loses the least if she's wrong. This freedom to roam across every market on earth is what draws a certain temperament to macro trading, and it's also what makes the strategy so hard, because a wider set of choices means more ways to be wrong.

There's a humility that experienced macro traders develop, and it comes from how often the economy defies confident predictions. The global system is staggeringly complex, shaped by politics, psychology, and random events that no model fully captures. A trader can be completely right about an economic imbalance and still lose money because the correction takes years longer than expected, or because a central bank intervenes to prevent it, or because some unrelated shock scrambles everything.

The best macro traders hold their views strongly but loosely, ready to change their minds when the facts change, because the alternative, marrying a thesis and refusing to abandon it as losses mount, has destroyed many talented people. Conviction without flexibility is fatal in a domain this unpredictable.

Currency and Interest Rate Positioning

Two instruments dominate global macro trading above all others: currencies and interest rates. They're where the biggest macro bets get made, partly because they're the most direct expression of a country's economic condition and partly because the markets for them are so enormous that even the largest funds can trade freely without moving prices against themselves.

Currencies deserve first attention because the foreign exchange market is the largest financial market on the planet, with trading volume measured in trillions of dollars every single day. A currency's value reflects the collective judgment of the world about a country's economy, and it moves on a handful of forces the macro trader watches closely. Interest rates are chief among them: when a country raises rates, its currency often strengthens, because higher rates attract foreign money seeking better returns, and that inflow of capital bids up the currency. Trade flows matter too, since a country that exports more than it imports sees demand for its currency from foreign buyers. Capital flows, political stability, and the actions of central banks all push currencies around, and the macro trader tries to anticipate these moves before they happen.

One particular currency strategy, the carry trade, deserves explanation because it's among the most widely used and most treacherous. The carry trade works by borrowing money in a currency with low interest rates and investing it in a currency with high interest rates, pocketing the difference in yield. For years, traders borrowed Japanese yen, where interest rates sat near zero, and invested in currencies like the Australian dollar or various emerging-market currencies paying much higher rates. As long as the exchange rates stayed stable, the trader collected the interest rate gap as pure profit. The strategy can run smoothly for a long time, lulling everyone into complacency, which is exactly what makes it dangerous. When markets turn volatile, the high-yielding currencies often fall sharply and the borrowed low-yield currency strengthens, so the trader loses on the exchange rate far more than she earned in interest. Carry trades tend to make small, steady profits for extended periods and then suffer sudden, violent losses, a pattern that has caught countless traders unprepared.

The single most celebrated macro trade in history was a currency bet, and it captures everything about how this strategy works at its best. In 1992, the British pound was part of a European exchange rate system that required Britain to keep its currency within a fixed band against other European currencies. George Soros, through his Quantum Fund, with Stanley Druckenmiller serving as the portfolio manager executing the trade, concluded that Britain couldn't sustain this commitment. The British economy was weak, and holding the pound at its required level demanded high interest rates the country couldn't afford. Soros saw an imbalance that had to break: the pound was propped up above its natural value, and something had to give.

He bet against it, and he bet enormous. The Quantum Fund built a massive short position against the pound, borrowing pounds and selling them, wagering that Britain would eventually be forced to abandon the fixed rate and let its currency fall. As pressure mounted, the British government fought back, raising interest rates and spending billions of its reserves buying pounds to defend the exchange rate. It wasn't enough. On September 16, 1992, a day the British press called Black Wednesday, Britain gave up, withdrew from the exchange rate system, and let the pound collapse. Soros's fund reportedly earned around a billion dollars in a matter of days, and he became known as the man who broke the Bank of England. The trade is studied to this day because it shows the macro approach in its purest form: identify an economic imbalance a government is trying to deny, bet heavily that reality will win, and profit when the dam finally bursts.

Interest rates are the other great macro instrument, and they're bound up tightly with currencies because central banks control both the level of rates and, indirectly, the value of the currency. A macro trader who forms a view about where interest rates are heading has several ways to bet on it. She can trade government bonds, whose prices fall when rates rise and rise when rates fall, an inverse relationship that's fundamental to fixed-income markets. She can trade interest rate futures directly, betting on the specific path rates will take. She can position along the yield curve, which is the relationship between short-term and long-term interest rates, betting that the gap between them will widen or narrow.

The relationship between bond prices and interest rates confuses many newcomers, so it's worth stating plainly.

When Interest Rates...	Bond Prices...	Why
Rise	Fall	Existing bonds paying old, lower rates become less attractive than new bonds
Fall	Rise	Existing bonds paying old, higher rates become more attractive than new bonds

This inverse relationship is the foundation of every interest rate bet. A trader who believes a central bank will raise rates more than the market expects can short government bonds, profiting as their prices fall. The year 2022 offered a textbook example. As inflation surged, the Federal Reserve began raising interest rates aggressively, faster and higher than most investors had anticipated. Macro traders who correctly foresaw this raised-rate environment and positioned against bonds made substantial money, while investors caught holding bonds suffered one of the worst years in the history of the bond market. The traders who won weren't lucky. They'd read the inflation data, understood that the Fed would have to respond forcefully, and bet on rising rates before the consensus caught up.

Central banks are the great movers of both currencies and interest rates, which makes reading them the central preoccupation of macro trading. When a central bank shifts its policy, it sends waves through every connected market. Macro traders study every speech, every meeting, every economic projection a central bank releases, hunting for clues about its next move. A trader who correctly anticipates a central bank's decision before the rest of the market can position ahead of the crowd and profit as everyone else adjusts. This is why so much macro analysis reduces to a single question: what will the central banks do next, and how does that differ from what the market currently expects? The gap between reality and expectation is where the money is made.

Trend-Following and Systematic CTAs

A large branch of the futures world abandons economic analysis entirely and bets on a single, stubborn observation about markets: things that have been going up tend to keep going up, and things that have been going down tend to keep going down. This is trend-following, and it powers most of what the industry calls managed futures, run by firms known as CTAs.

The name CTA stands for Commodity Trading Advisor, a regulatory label from the United States that's badly outdated, because these firms trade far more than commodities. A modern CTA might have positions in currencies, government bonds, interest rate futures, stock index futures, and commodities all at once, spread across dozens or even hundreds of markets around the world. The "commodity" in the name is a historical artifact from when these traders focused on agricultural and raw-material futures. Today the label just means a fund that trades futures contracts systematically, and the strategy inside most of them is trend-following.

The logic of trend-following is almost embarrassingly simple, which is part of why skeptics doubt it works and believers find it beautiful. The trend-follower doesn't try to predict anything. She doesn't analyze whether a currency is overvalued or whether a central bank will cut rates. She simply observes which markets are moving in a sustained direction and rides them. If wheat has been climbing for three months, she buys wheat and holds it as long as the climb continues. If the Japanese yen has been falling steadily, she shorts the yen and stays short until the fall stops. When a trend reverses, she exits and flips to the other side. She's not forecasting the future. She's identifying momentum that already exists and betting it persists a while longer.

Everything about this approach is systematic, meaning it runs on predefined rules executed by computers rather than on human judgment. The trader, or more accurately the team of researchers, builds a set of mathematical rules that define what counts as a trend, when to enter a position, how large to make it, and when to exit. Once the rules are set, the computer follows them without emotion, taking positions across every market the system covers. This mechanical discipline is the whole point. It removes the human tendencies that wreck most traders: the fear that makes you sell winners too early, the hope that makes you hold losers too long, the ego that makes you cling to a losing bet rather than admit you're wrong. The machine feels none of this. It follows the rules.

Detection through risk control run with no human intervention

The origins of systematic trend-following include one of the most famous experiments in trading history. In the early 1980s, two traders named Richard Dennis and William Eckhardt made a bet with each other about whether great trading could be taught or was an innate gift. Dennis believed it could be taught to anyone. To settle the argument, he recruited a group of ordinary people with no trading background, gave them a set of mechanical trend-following rules, and funded them with real money. He called them the Turtles. The experiment worked remarkably well. Many of the Turtles went on to earn large profits following the systematic rules Dennis taught them, and several built successful careers as traders. The lesson resonated through the industry: a disciplined, rules-based trend-following system, followed faithfully, could produce results without any special intuition or forecasting genius. The edge was in the discipline, not in prediction.

Why should such a simple approach work at all? The answer lies in human behavior and how information spreads through markets. When news breaks that should move a price, the price doesn't jump instantly to its new correct level. Instead it drifts there over days, weeks, or months, as different investors absorb the information at different speeds and react gradually. Some traders pile in as a trend develops, extending it. Herding behavior, where investors follow the crowd, pushes trends further than fundamentals alone would justify. These behavioral patterns create the sustained directional moves that trend-followers capture. The trend exists because people are slow, emotional, and imitative, and the systematic trader profits from that predictable human messiness without needing to understand any particular market.

Trend-following has one property that makes it genuinely valuable inside a broader portfolio, and it appears at the worst moments for everyone else. When a real crisis hits, markets often move in large, sustained directions as panic sets in: stocks fall for weeks, safe-haven bonds rise, commodities crater. These sustained moves are exactly what trend-following systems are built to capture. As a result, managed futures funds frequently make money during market crashes, when almost everything else is losing. This tendency to profit in crises has earned the strategy a reputation as a portfolio protector. In 2008, as stock markets collapsed around the world, many trend-following CTAs had one of their best years ever, riding the sustained downward moves in stocks and the upward moves in bonds. The same thing happened in 2022, when trend-followers profited handsomely by being short bonds and long commodities as inflation drove those sustained trends.

Here's how managed futures behaved across several notable periods, which shows both the strategy's crisis strength and its weakness.

Period	Market Environment	Trend-Following Result
2008 financial crisis	Stocks crashed, strong sustained trends	Excellent, one of the best years on record
2010-2019 bull market	Choppy, trendless in many stretches	Mediocre, long flat periods frustrated investors
2022 inflation shock	Bonds fell, commodities rose, clear trends	Excellent, a standout year
Calm, range-bound markets	Prices oscillate without direction	Poor, repeated small losses from false signals

The weakness is as real as the strength, and it sits in that second and fourth row. Trend-following struggles badly in markets that move sideways without sustained direction. When prices oscillate up and down in a range, the system keeps detecting trends that immediately reverse, buying just before a drop and selling just before a rise, bleeding money through a series of false signals called whipsaws.

The 2010s were painful for many trend-followers precisely because markets, supported by central bank intervention, often drifted and chopped rather than trending cleanly. Investors who'd loaded up on managed futures after the strategy's triumph in 2008 grew frustrated watching it languish for years afterward. This is the trend-follower's burden: the strategy shines in crises and sustained moves but suffers through the long, directionless stretches in between, and an investor has to endure those lean years to be present for the crisis years when the strategy pays off.

The diversification value is the deeper reason sophisticated investors hold managed futures despite the frustrating flat periods. Because trend-following makes money in a different way than stocks and bonds, and especially because it tends to profit when stocks are crashing, it provides a return stream that behaves independently of a traditional portfolio. An investor who owns stocks and bonds and adds a trend-following allocation gains a component that zigs when the rest zags, particularly during the market disasters that do the most damage. The value isn't that trend-following earns spectacular returns on its own, because over long stretches its returns can be modest. The value is that those returns arrive on a different schedule than everything else, cushioning the portfolio when other assets are collapsing together.

David Harding, who founded Winton Group, and the team at Man AHL built large businesses on this systematic approach, applying rigorous mathematics and vast computing power to trend-following across global futures markets. These firms employ armies of researchers, physicists and mathematicians and programmers, all working to refine the rules that define and capture trends.

The strategy has grown more sophisticated over the decades, incorporating more markets, more nuanced signals, and better risk controls, but the core idea remains what Richard Dennis taught his Turtles: find the trend, ride it with discipline, cut the position when the trend ends, and never let emotion override the system. And now, it's commonly available in ETF form such that retail investors have easy access.

Discretionary vs. Systematic Macro Approaches

The macro world splits into two philosophical camps, and the divide between them runs deeper than technique. It's a disagreement about whether human judgment or mechanical rules produce better decisions, and it shapes everything about how a fund operates.

The discretionary camp puts a human being in charge of every decision. A discretionary macro trader like George Soros, Stanley Druckenmiller, Paul Tudor Jones, or Louis Bacon studies the world, forms views, and makes bets based on judgment, experience, and intuition. When the discretionary trader sees an opportunity, she sizes the position according to her conviction and her read of the situation. She can react instantly to a surprise, weigh factors no model captures, and change her mind when something feels wrong. Her edge is the accumulated wisdom and pattern recognition that comes from years of watching markets, an intuition that lets her sense when an imbalance is about to break or when a trade has stopped making sense.

The systematic camp removes the human from individual decisions entirely. A systematic macro fund, like the trend-following CTAs already discussed and many others, encodes its investment logic into computer models that make every trade according to predefined rules. The humans build and refine the models, but they don't override them trade by trade. The systematic approach prizes consistency and discipline, arguing that human judgment is unreliable, prone to emotion, fatigue, and bias, while a well-designed model applies the same sound logic every single time without wavering.

Each approach has genuine strengths and genuine weaknesses, and neither is simply better than the other. Here's how they compare on the dimensions that matter most.

Dimension	Discretionary	Systematic
Who decides	A human, using judgment	A computer, following rules
Reacting to novel events	Excellent, can adapt to anything	Poor, only knows what it was built for
Emotional discipline	Vulnerable to fear, greed, ego	Immune, follows rules mechanically
Consistency	Varies with the trader's state	Identical every time
Scalability	Limited by one person's capacity	Scales easily across many markets
Key-person risk	High, the fund depends on one mind	Low, the system outlives individuals
Testing before use	Can't rigorously backtest a hunch	Can be tested against decades of history

Look at the row on novel events, because it captures the deepest difference. A discretionary trader can respond to something that's never happened before, drawing on judgment to navigate a genuinely new situation, a pandemic, a war, a financial innovation with no precedent. A systematic model can only respond to the kinds of situations it was built to handle. When something truly unprecedented occurs, outside the range of anything in its historical data, the model can behave unpredictably or fail, because it's applying rules derived from a past that no longer resembles the present. The discretionary trader's adaptability is her great advantage in exactly these moments.

But the row on emotional discipline cuts the other way, and it's the systematic camp's strongest argument. Human traders are notoriously bad at controlling their emotions when real money is on the line. They hold losing positions too long because admitting a mistake hurts. They sell winning positions too early because they're afraid of giving back profits. They get overconfident after a win and reckless after a loss. They freeze in a crisis. A systematic model does none of this. It executes its rules with perfect indifference, buying when the rules say buy even when doing so feels terrifying, selling when the rules say sell even when every instinct screams to hold. This emotional discipline, this freedom from the psychological weaknesses that sabotage human traders, is the systematic approach's central claim to superiority.

Key-person risk is a practical concern that pushes many large investors toward systematic funds. A discretionary macro fund built around a single brilliant trader has an obvious vulnerability: if that person retires, falls ill, loses their touch, or simply has a bad few years, the entire fund is in jeopardy, because everything depended on one mind. A systematic fund faces no such fragility. Its logic lives in the models, which continue working regardless of which individuals come and go. For a pension fund allocating money that must last for decades, a strategy that doesn't hinge on one irreplaceable human has real appeal.

The reality, as with most either-or debates in investing, is that the sharp line between the two camps has blurred. Many funds now blend both, using systematic models to generate ideas and screen opportunities while allowing human judgment to make final decisions or adjust the models in unusual conditions. Bridgewater, for instance, is heavily rules-based, encoding its economic logic into systematic processes, yet it maintains human oversight and judgment in how those rules are applied. Some discretionary traders use quantitative models as inputs to their thinking without surrendering final control. The question is no longer purely whether to trust humans or machines, but how to combine the adaptability and insight of human judgment with the discipline and consistency of systematic rules, capturing the strengths of each while limiting the weaknesses of both. The best funds have concluded that the two approaches aren't rivals so much as complementary tools, each suited to different parts of the problem.

Discussion Question

Systematic strategies win on discipline, applying sound rules without the emotion that wrecks human traders, but they can only respond to situations resembling their historical data, leaving them exposed when something genuinely unprecedented arrives. Discretionary traders can adapt to anything new, yet they carry all the emotional and psychological frailties that discipline is meant to remove. If you had to allocate your own money to one approach for the next twenty years, knowing that period will certainly contain events no model has seen before, which would you trust more, and what does your choice reveal about whether you fear human weakness or machine rigidity more?

Chapter 5: Event-Driven and Relative Value Strategies

The strategies covered so far all share a dependence on getting the future right in some broad sense: which stocks will rise, which economies will stumble, which way rates will move. Event-driven investing narrows the question to something far more specific and, in a way, more knowable. It bets on the outcome of particular corporate events, a merger closing, a bankrupt company reorganizing, a division being spun off, each with its own defined timeline and its own set of possible outcomes. The appeal is a return that depends less on the market's mood and more on whether a specific thing happens.

When two companies announce a merger, a curious gap almost always opens up. The acquirer offers to buy the target at a set price, yet the target's stock keeps trading a little below that price, right up until the deal actually closes. That gap is money sitting on the table for anyone willing to bet the deal goes through, and it's a disaster for anyone caught in it when the deal falls apart. Capturing gaps like this, across mergers, bankruptcies, restructurings, and every other corporate event that creates a temporary mispricing, is the business of the event-driven and relative value managers this chapter examines. The strategies range from the relatively straightforward to the genuinely intricate, but they share a common spirit: find a situation where the market has mispriced the outcome of a specific event, and position to profit when reality resolves.

Merger Arbitrage and Deal Spreads

Merger arbitrage is the flagship event-driven strategy, the one that defines the category, and its logic is clean enough to grasp in a single example.

Suppose Company A announces it will buy Company B for 50 dollars per share in cash. Before the announcement, Company B was trading at, say, 38 dollars. The moment the deal goes public, B's stock leaps upward, but here's the strange part: it doesn't jump all the way to 50. It settles at something like 47. There's a persistent gap, three dollars in this case, between where the target trades and the price the acquirer has agreed to pay. That gap is called the deal spread, and it exists for a specific reason. The market isn't certain the deal will actually close. Deals fall apart. Regulators block them, financing collapses, shareholders vote no, or one side simply walks away. The three-dollar gap is the market's way of pricing that uncertainty. If completion were guaranteed, the stock would trade right at 50.

The merger arbitrageur steps into this gap. She buys Company B at 47, betting the deal closes and the stock rises to 50, delivering her a three-dollar profit per share. If she's right, and most announced deals do eventually close, she captures that spread. The percentage looks small, three dollars on a 47-dollar stock is about 6.4 percent, but the magic is in the timeline. If the deal closes in three months, she's earned 6.4

percent in a quarter of a year, which annualizes to something far more attractive. And here's what makes the strategy genuinely appealing: that return has almost nothing to do with the stock market. Whether the broader market rises or falls over those three months, her profit depends only on whether this particular deal closes. She's captured a return stream disconnected from the market's direction, which is exactly the kind of decorrelated profit sophisticated investors prize.

Here's the arithmetic of a deal spread laid out, because seeing the annualization makes clear why arbitrageurs bother with such thin-looking gaps.

Element	Value
Acquirer's offer price	$50.00
Target's current price	$47.00
Deal spread	$3.00, or 6.4%
Expected time to close	3 months
Annualized return if deal closes	roughly 26%
Loss if deal breaks and stock falls to $38	$9.00, or about 19%

Study that bottom row, because it reveals the true nature of merger arbitrage and why it's harder than it first appears. The upside is capped and modest: three dollars, no more, because the acquirer won't pay above 50. The downside, if the deal collapses, is severe: the stock crashes back toward where it traded before the announcement, or lower, wiping out far more than the spread ever offered. This asymmetry defines the strategy. A merger arbitrageur wins small amounts frequently and loses large amounts rarely. The profits accumulate quietly, deal after deal, and then a single broken deal can erase months of gains in a day. The whole enterprise depends on being right about deal completion the overwhelming majority of the time, because the math punishes each failure so heavily.

This means the merger arbitrageur's real job isn't spotting the spread, which anyone can see, but assessing the probability that the deal actually closes. That assessment is where skill lives. She has to understand why deals break, and there are several main reasons.

Regulatory rejection is the largest threat to big deals. Governments review mergers for antitrust concerns, whether combining the two companies would harm competition, and they can block or force changes to deals they don't like. National security reviews can kill deals involving foreign buyers or sensitive industries. When AT&T agreed to buy Time Warner in 2016, the Department of Justice sued to block it on antitrust grounds, and the deal spread widened dramatically as the market grew uncertain, before a court eventually allowed the merger to proceed in 2018. Arbitrageurs who correctly judged the deal would survive the legal challenge profited; those who panicked and sold at the wide spread locked in losses. When the Trump administration blocked Broadcom's attempt to buy Qualcomm in 2018 on national security grounds, that deal died entirely, and anyone positioned for its completion suffered.

Financing failure can sink a deal when the acquirer can't raise the money it promised. Shareholder rejection happens when the target's owners vote down the deal, often because they think the price is too low. And a category of contract clauses called material adverse change provisions can let an acquirer walk away if something dramatically bad happens to the target between signing and closing. Each of these is a way the three-dollar spread turns into a nine-dollar loss.

The strategy also comes in different forms depending on how the acquirer is paying. In a cash deal, like the example above, the acquirer pays a fixed dollar amount, and the arbitrage is straightforward: buy the target and wait. In a stock deal, the acquirer pays with its own shares rather than cash, offering, say, half a share of Company A for each share of Company B. This complicates things, because now the value the target's shareholders receive fluctuates with Company A's stock price. To arbitrage a stock deal, the manager buys the target and simultaneously shorts the acquirer's stock in the right proportion, locking in the spread regardless of how the acquirer's shares move. The short position hedges away the risk that the acquirer's stock falls and drags down the deal's value.

Merger arbitrage has a long and slightly notorious history. In its early decades it was called risk arbitrage, and one of its most famous practitioners was Ivan Boesky, who became enormously wealthy trading merger situations in the 1980s. It later emerged that a good deal of Boesky's success came from illegal insider trading, buying targets based on advance knowledge of deals that hadn't been announced yet. His conviction in 1986 became one of the defining scandals of Wall Street's excess, and it cast a long shadow over the strategy, though legitimate merger arbitrage, based on public information and careful analysis, remained a respectable and widely practiced approach. John Paulson, who later became famous for betting against the housing market, built his early career on merger arbitrage.

A recent example shows the strategy under maximum stress. When Microsoft agreed to buy the video game company Activision Blizzard in early 2022 for 95 dollars per share, the deal faced ferocious regulatory opposition. The Federal Trade Commission in the United States sued to block it, and Britain's competition regulator initially rejected it outright. For well over a year, Activision's stock traded far below the 95-dollar offer, sometimes in the mid-70s, reflecting deep market doubt that the deal would ever close. The spread was enormous, offering a large return to anyone confident the merger would survive. Arbitrageurs split sharply on the odds. Those who studied the regulatory arguments closely and concluded Microsoft would ultimately prevail held their positions through months of frightening headlines. When the deal finally closed in October 2023, those investors collected a substantial profit, while the doubters who'd sold missed it entirely. The episode captured the essence of merger arbitrage: the money goes to whoever reads the probability of completion most accurately, and that reading requires genuine expertise in law, regulation, and corporate behavior, not just the ability to spot a gap.

Distressed Debt and Bankruptcy Investing

When a company slides toward failure, most investors flee. Distressed debt investors move toward the wreckage, buying the bonds and loans of troubled companies at steep discounts, precisely because everyone else is desperate to sell. The strategy is built on a willingness to analyze situations others find too frightening or too complicated to touch, and it operates in a corner of finance governed by the specialized rules of bankruptcy.

The starting point is understanding what a distressed investor is actually buying. When a company borrows money, it issues debt, bonds and loans that promise to pay lenders back with interest. As long as the company is healthy, this debt trades near its full value, its face value, because everyone expects to be repaid. But when a company runs into serious trouble and default looks likely, its debt plummets in price. A bond that promises to pay back 100 dollars might trade for 40 dollars, or 20, or even less, because the market doubts the company can pay in full. The distressed investor buys these deeply discounted claims, betting that they'll ultimately be worth more than the depressed price she paid, either because the company recovers or because the assets backing the debt are worth more than the market currently believes.

To understand why some distressed debt is a smart buy and other distressed debt is worthless, you have to understand the order in which claims get paid when a company fails. Bankruptcy law establishes a strict hierarchy, called the priority of claims or the absolute priority rule, that determines who gets paid first from whatever value remains. This waterfall is the single most important concept in distressed investing.

Priority Rank	Claim Type	Typical Recovery in Bankruptcy
First	Secured creditors (debt backed by specific assets)	Often high, sometimes full
Second	Senior unsecured creditors	Moderate, varies widely
Third	Subordinated (junior) creditors	Low, often pennies on the dollar
Fourth	Preferred shareholders	Usually little to nothing
Last	Common shareholders	Almost always wiped out entirely

Read this waterfall from the top down and the strategy's logic becomes clear. When a company's value is carved up in bankruptcy, the secured creditors at the top get paid first, in full if there's enough value to cover them. Then whatever's left flows to the next tier, and the next, until the value runs out. Everyone below that point gets nothing. Common shareholders, sitting at the very bottom, are almost always wiped out completely, which is why owning the stock of a bankrupt company is usually a bet on zero. The distressed investor's craft is figuring out where in this waterfall the company's remaining value runs dry, and buying the claims that sit just above that line, the ones that will get paid while the claims below them won't.

There's a name for the security sitting right at that critical point: the fulcrum security. It's the layer of debt where the company's value runs out, meaning the holders of that security get partially repaid and often end up converting their claims into ownership of the reorganized company. Identifying the fulcrum security is the central analytical challenge in distressed investing, because owning it can mean ending up in control of the business itself.

This leads to one of the most aggressive distressed strategies, known as loan-to-own. Rather than simply betting a distressed bond will recover in price, the investor buys the fulcrum debt with the specific intention of converting it into equity ownership when the company reorganizes. Companies in serious distress often go through Chapter 11 bankruptcy, a legal process that lets a company restructure its debts and continue operating rather than shutting down. In a typical reorganization, the old shareholders are wiped out, and the creditors, especially those holding the fulcrum security, receive new stock in the reorganized company in exchange for forgiving the old debt. An investor who bought that fulcrum debt cheaply can emerge from the bankruptcy owning a controlling stake in a company that's now shed its crushing debt load and can operate profitably again. She bought debt but ended up owning the business, at a fraction of what the business is worth cleaned up.

The distinction between Chapter 11 and Chapter 7 matters here. Chapter 11 is reorganization: the company survives, restructures its obligations, and keeps operating, which is where loan-to-own strategies play out. Chapter 7 is liquidation: the company shuts down entirely, its assets are sold off, and the proceeds are distributed to creditors according to the priority waterfall. Distressed investors analyze which path a troubled company is likely to take, because it changes everything about what their claims will be worth.

The people who practice this strategy have earned a colorful, slightly menacing reputation, sometimes called vulture investors for their habit of feeding on dying companies. Howard Marks built Oaktree Capital into one of the largest distressed debt firms in the world, and his patient, analytical approach to buying quality assets at distressed prices made him one of the most respected investors of his era. Distressed investing tends to have its greatest opportunities during economic crises, when defaults spike and troubled debt floods the market at fire-sale prices. The firms that kept cash ready during the good times could deploy it aggressively during the 2008 crisis, buying distressed claims at prices that later delivered enormous returns as the economy recovered.

Some distressed situations become legendary for their sheer tenacity. Paul Singer's Elliott Management spent years pursuing the government of Argentina over defaulted sovereign debt. After Argentina defaulted in 2001, most creditors accepted a restructuring that paid them a fraction of what they were owed. Elliott refused, holding out for full payment and pursuing Argentina through courts around the world. The fight grew so aggressive that in 2012, Elliott persuaded a court in Ghana to detain an Argentine naval training ship, the ARA Libertad, as collateral for the unpaid debt. The standoff lasted more than a decade before Argentina finally settled in 2016, delivering Elliott a large profit on debt it had bought cheaply. The saga captured the distressed investor's defining trait: a willingness to fight, wait, and endure complexity that would exhaust anyone else, all in pursuit of value hidden inside a situation others had given up on.

Convertible Bond Arbitrage

Some hedge fund strategies exist to exploit the mispricing of a single, peculiar financial instrument, and convertible bond arbitrage is built around one of the most useful hybrids in finance: the convertible bond.

A convertible bond is a bond with a twist. Like any bond, it pays interest and promises to return its face value at maturity. But it carries an additional feature: the holder can choose to convert the bond into a set number of shares of the company's stock. This makes a convertible two things bundled together. It's a bond, providing steady interest and a claim on the company ahead of shareholders, and it's also an option on the stock, because if the stock rises high enough, the holder can convert and capture the gain. Companies issue convertibles because the embedded conversion option lets them pay a lower interest rate than they'd owe on a plain bond, since investors accept less interest in exchange for the potential stock upside.

The arbitrage opportunity arises because convertible bonds are complicated to value, and complicated instruments often get mispriced. Buried inside every convertible is that option on the stock, and options have a value that depends on the stock's price, its volatility, interest rates, and time. When the market prices a convertible bond, it has to price that embedded option, and it frequently gets the pricing wrong, often making the option cheaper than it should be. The convertible arbitrageur's core bet is that she can buy this embedded option at a discount and hedge away the risks she doesn't want, keeping only the mispricing as profit.

Here's how the trade works in practice. The arbitrageur buys the convertible bond, which gives her exposure to the stock through the conversion feature, along with the bond's interest payments. Then she shorts the underlying stock in a carefully calculated amount. This short position hedges out her exposure to the stock's direction. If the stock falls, she loses a little on the convertible but gains on her short, and the two roughly offset. If the stock rises, she gains on the convertible's conversion value but loses on her short. The point of the hedge is to neutralize the effect of the stock's direction so that her profit comes from other sources: the interest the bond pays, the interest she earns on the cash from her short sale, and, above all, the volatility of the stock.

The behavior of this position across different stock moves is worth laying out, because it shows how the hedge is supposed to produce profit regardless of direction.

Stock Movement	Convertible Bond	Short Stock Position	Net Effect
Stock rises sharply	Gains value via conversion option	Loses value	Manager adjusts hedge, profits from volatility
Stock falls sharply	Loses some value, cushioned by bond floor	Gains value	Manager adjusts hedge, profits from volatility
Stock stays flat	Collects interest, holds value	Collects short interest	Steady income, low excitement

The real engine of profit is a technique called delta hedging, which involves constantly adjusting the size of the short position as the stock moves. When the stock rises, the convertible's option feature becomes more sensitive to the stock, so the arbitrageur increases her short. When the stock falls, she reduces it. Done well, this continuous rebalancing lets her profit from the stock bouncing around, from its volatility, regardless of which direction it ultimately goes. A volatile stock generates more trading profit through this rebalancing than a calm one, which is why convertible arbitrageurs love volatility and why they're really making a bet on volatility more than on the company itself.

Ken Griffin built Citadel, now one of the largest and most successful hedge fund firms in existence, starting largely from convertible bond arbitrage. As a Harvard undergraduate in the late 1980s, Griffin began trading convertible bonds from his dorm room, exploiting exactly the kind of mispricing described here. That early focus on the mathematical relationships inside convertible securities grew into a firm managing tens of billions of dollars across many strategies. The origin story illustrates how a narrow, technical edge, understanding convertibles better than the market priced them, could serve as the foundation for an enormous business.

Convertible arbitrage carries a dangerous vulnerability, though, and it revealed itself catastrophically in 2008. The strategy depends heavily on borrowing to amplify what are usually small mispricings, and it depends on being able to short the underlying stocks. When the financial crisis hit, both of these supports collapsed at once. Lenders pulled back the borrowed money that convertible arbitrageurs relied on, forcing them to sell their convertible bonds into a falling market. At the same time, regulators, panicking about market stability, temporarily banned short selling of many financial stocks, which destroyed the hedges that convertible arbitrageurs needed to protect their positions. The strategy suffered enormous losses in 2008, with many convertible arbitrage funds losing a third or more of their value as the whole approach unwound simultaneously across the industry. The episode taught a hard lesson about strategies that look low-risk in calm conditions but depend on borrowing and short selling that can vanish exactly when they're needed most.

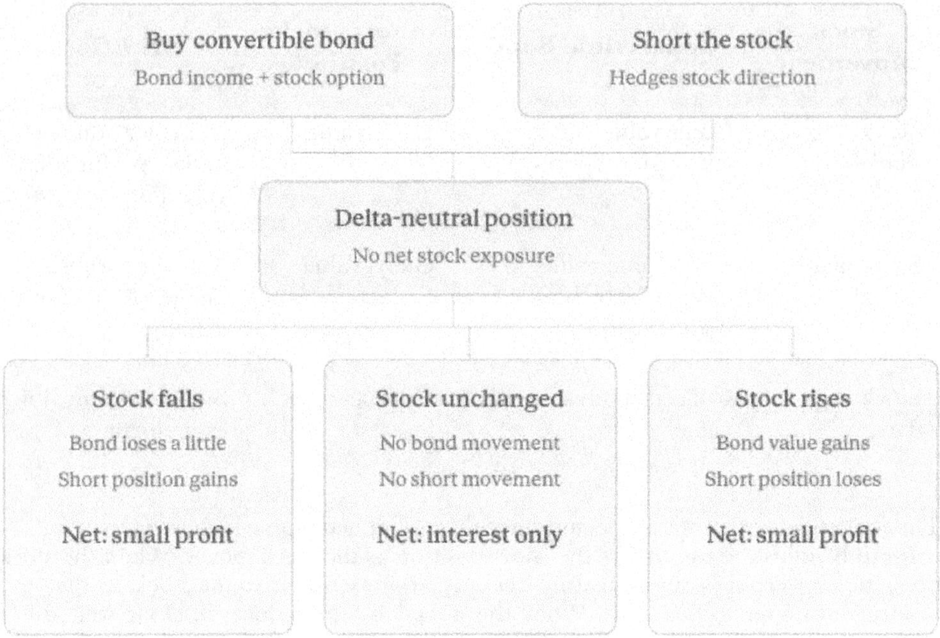

Profit comes from volatility and rebalancing, not from direction

Capital Structure Arbitrage

A single company issues many different securities: senior bonds, junior bonds, various loans, preferred stock, common stock, and sometimes derivatives tied to its debt. Each of these represents a different claim on the same underlying business, and in theory their prices should all tell a consistent story about the company's health. In practice they sometimes don't, and capital structure arbitrage exists to profit when the different pieces of a company's capital structure contradict each other.

The core idea is that all of a company's securities are ultimately claims on the same set of assets and cash flows, so they should be priced in a coherent relationship to one another. The stock and the bonds are both betting on the same company, just with different risk and different priority. When the market prices these securities inconsistently, when the stock implies the company is doing fine while the bonds imply it's headed for trouble, an arbitrageur can bet that the inconsistency will resolve. She goes long the security she thinks is underpriced and short the one she thinks is overpriced, both issued by the same company, profiting when their relationship snaps back to something sensible.

This works because different investors trade different parts of a company's capital structure, and they don't always agree or communicate. Stock investors and bond investors are often entirely separate groups, watching different signals and reacting at different speeds. Credit default swaps, which are contracts that pay out if a company defaults on its debt, add another security whose price reflects the market's view of default risk, and it too can drift out of line with the stock. The capital structure arbitrageur watches all these related securities and pounces when they tell contradictory stories, betting the contradiction can't last.

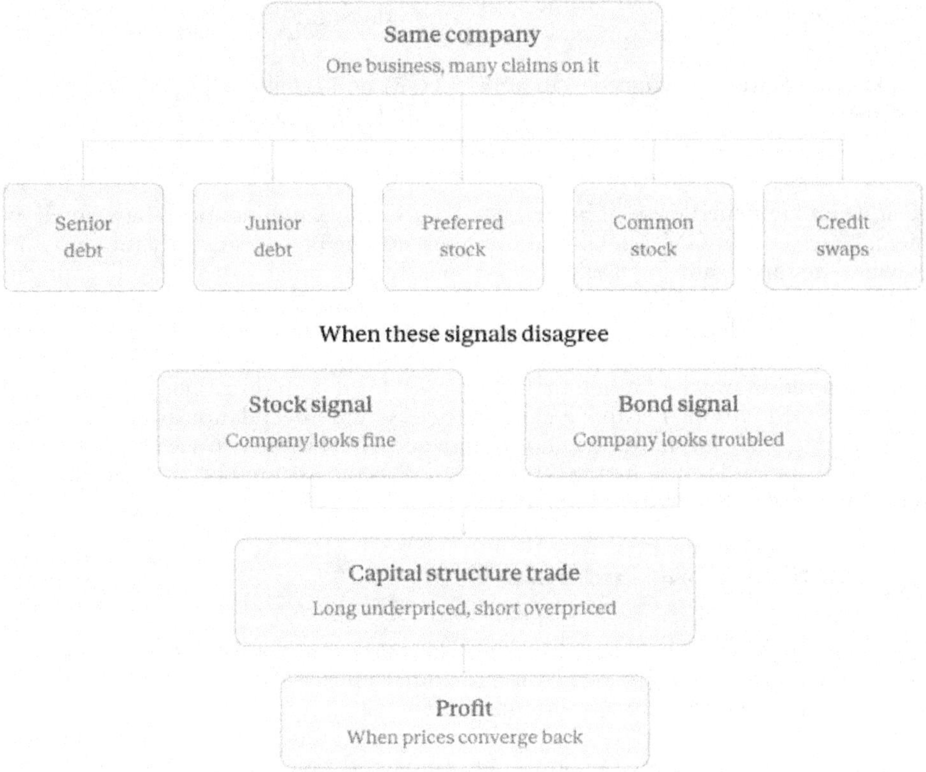

The intellectual foundation for this strategy comes from a model developed by the economist Robert Merton, which treats a company's stock as essentially an option on the company's assets. Under this framework, the stock, the debt, and the default risk are all mathematically linked, because they all derive from the same underlying business value. If you can price one accurately, the model tells you what the others should be worth, and any deviation is a potential trade. This theoretical link is what gives capital structure arbitrageurs the confidence to bet that misaligned securities will converge.

The strategy sounds elegant, and it can be treacherous, as a famous 2005 episode demonstrated. Many hedge funds had put on a popular capital structure trade involving General Motors: they were long GM's bonds and short GM's stock. The logic seemed sound. They believed GM was in gradual decline, so the stock should fall, while the bonds, higher in the priority waterfall, would hold their value better. It was a bet on the relationship between the two securities. Then two unexpected events struck within days of each other, and both legs of the trade blew up simultaneously.

Event	Effect on the Trade
Kirk Kerkorian announced a tender offer to buy GM stock	GM stock jumped up, causing losses on the short position
GM's bonds were downgraded to junk status	GM bonds fell sharply, causing losses on the long position

Read what happened there. The investor Kirk Kerkorian announced he wanted to buy a large stake in GM, which sent the stock surging upward, exactly the opposite of what the funds shorting it expected. At nearly the same moment, credit rating agencies downgraded GM's bonds to junk status, sending the bonds tumbling, again the opposite of what the funds holding them expected. Both sides of the supposedly hedged trade moved the wrong way at once. Funds that thought they'd constructed a low-risk position watched it hemorrhage money from both directions simultaneously. The 2005 GM episode became a cautionary lesson in how relationships that appear stable and logical can shatter when unforeseen events hit the two securities in opposite ways, and how a hedge is only as good as the assumption that the two legs remain related in the expected manner.

Special Situations and Spin-Offs

The final category is the widest, a catch-all for corporate events that create opportunities without fitting neatly into the other buckets. Special situations investing covers any unusual corporate event that temporarily mispriced a security: restructurings, rights offerings, liquidations, litigation, tender offers, and the addition or removal of a stock from a major index, among others. The unifying thread is that a specific corporate event, rather than the company's ongoing business or the market's direction, drives the opportunity.

Spin-offs are the most studied special situation, and they contain a genuine and persistent market inefficiency worth understanding. A spin-off happens when a company separates one of its divisions into an independent, publicly traded company, distributing shares of the new company to its existing shareholders. If you own stock in the parent company, you suddenly receive shares in the newly independent business, whether you wanted them or not. That involuntary distribution is the source of the opportunity.

Here's why spin-offs tend to be mispriced right after they happen. The shareholders who receive the new spin-off shares frequently didn't want them. An investor who bought the parent company for its main business has no interest in a small, unfamiliar division that's just landed in their account, so they sell it, often immediately and without regard to price. Index funds are sometimes forced to sell spin-off shares because the new company doesn't belong to the index they track. Large institutions may dump the shares because the position is too small to bother analyzing. This wave of indiscriminate selling, driven by the mechanics of the distribution rather than by any judgment about the spin-off's value, pushes the new company's stock below what it's actually worth. An investor who does the analysis everyone else is skipping can buy the spun-off company cheaply in those early days before the market properly values it.

Joel Greenblatt, who ran Gotham Capital to extraordinary returns, wrote extensively about this pattern and made spin-offs a centerpiece of his approach. His insight was that the forced, price-insensitive selling around spin-offs created reliable bargains for anyone willing to do the work of valuing the new companies. He also observed that spun-off companies often perform well as independent businesses, freed from a corporate parent that may have neglected or mismanaged them, and now run by management teams whose incentives are tied directly to the smaller company's success. The combination of temporary underpricing and improved operational focus made spin-offs one of the more dependable sources of opportunity he found.

Real examples abound. When eBay spun off PayPal as an independent company in 2015, PayPal went on to become far more valuable than many expected, rewarding investors who recognized its potential as a standalone payments business. When Abbott Laboratories spun off AbbVie, its pharmaceutical division, the newly independent company grew into a major drug maker in its own right. In each case, separating the division from its parent let the market value it properly for the first time, and early investors who saw the value before the crowd did captured the gains.

Special situations investing rewards a particular temperament: patience, attention to detail, and a willingness to analyze obscure corporate events that most investors ignore because they seem too small, too complicated, or too boring. The opportunities tend to be modest in size and specific in nature, which keeps larger investors away and leaves room for those willing to dig into the details of a rights offering or a complex restructuring. What ties special situations to everything else in this chapter is the underlying principle: a specific corporate event has created a temporary gap between a security's price and its true value, and the investor who understands the event better than the market can capture that gap when it closes.

Discussion Question

Every strategy in this chapter shares the same structural bargain: frequent small gains in exchange for the rare large loss when an event breaks the wrong way, whether a merger collapses, a hedge comes apart, or a distressed company recovers less than expected. This pattern of steady profits punctuated by sudden severe losses can make a manager look brilliantly consistent for years right up until the moment it doesn't. How should an investor tell the difference between an event-driven manager who's genuinely skilled at assessing probabilities and one who's simply been collecting small gains while the inevitable large loss hasn't happened yet, and can that difference even be known before the bad event arrives?

Chapter 6: Quantitative and Systematic Approaches

The strategies in earlier chapters all involved human judgment about specific situations, a manager deciding a stock was cheap, an economy was overheating, a merger would close. Quantitative investing removes that judgment and replaces it with mathematics, statistics, and computing power applied at enormous scale. A quant fund might hold thousands of positions at once, each one tiny, each selected not because a human likes the company but because a model identified a statistical pattern suggesting a small edge. The bet on any single position is nearly meaningless; the profit comes from making thousands of slightly favorable bets and letting the mathematics of large numbers work in the fund's favor. This chapter examines how these strategies function, from the statistical arbitrage that finds fleeting patterns in prices, to the factor investing that harvests known sources of return, to the machine learning now reshaping the field, and finally to the treacherous problem of testing these models without fooling yourself.

Statistical Arbitrage Models

Statistical arbitrage, universally shortened to stat arb, extends the pairs trading idea from an earlier chapter into something vastly larger and faster, powered entirely by computers finding patterns no human could track.

Recall the logic of pairs trading: find two similar stocks that normally move together, and when they temporarily diverge, bet they'll converge again. Statistical arbitrage takes this basic concept, that prices which have drifted apart tend to snap back into their normal relationship, and applies it across hundreds or thousands of securities simultaneously, using mathematical models to identify the relationships and computers to execute the trades. Instead of watching two stocks, a stat arb system monitors the relationships among an entire universe of stocks, hunting for any that have moved out of their statistically normal alignment and positioning to profit when they revert.

The foundational concept underneath most stat arb is mean reversion, the tendency of prices to return to an average level after straying from it. A stat arb model studies the historical relationships between securities and establishes what's normal, then watches for deviations from that norm. When a stock moves unusually far from where the model says it should be relative to similar stocks, the system bets on a return to normal, buying the ones that have fallen too far and shorting the ones that have risen too far. The bet isn't that any particular stock is good or bad. It's purely that an abnormal relationship will normalize, a statistical regularity the model has observed thousands of times in historical data.

What makes stat arb distinctive is the scale and speed at which it operates. A human pairs trader might follow a dozen relationships and trade a few times a week. A stat arb system tracks thousands of relationships and trades constantly, entering and exiting positions in minutes or seconds, holding each one only as long as the statistical edge persists. Because any single trade offers a minuscule expected profit, the strategy requires enormous numbers of trades to accumulate meaningful returns. The whole approach rests on the law of large numbers: each individual bet is barely better than a coin flip, but make enough of these slightly favorable bets and the aggregate outcome becomes reliably profitable, in the same way a casino profits not from any single spin of the roulette wheel but from the small, consistent edge multiplied across millions of spins.

Here's how statistical arbitrage compares to the human pairs trading it evolved from, which clarifies what the computerization actually changed.

Feature	Manual Pairs Trading	Statistical Arbitrage
Number of relationships tracked	A handful	Thousands, simultaneously
Speed of execution	Days or weeks	Seconds to minutes
Decision maker	Human judgment	Mathematical model
Number of trades	Few	Enormous, continuous
Source of profit	Large moves in a few pairs	Tiny edges across many positions
Holding period	Weeks to months	Minutes to days

The origins of statistical arbitrage trace back to the same Morgan Stanley quantitative group mentioned earlier, where researchers in the 1980s developed the first systematic versions of the strategy. As computing power grew cheaper and faster through the 1990s and 2000s, stat arb became one of the dominant strategies among quantitative hedge funds, with firms competing to find subtler patterns and execute them faster than rivals. The competition itself created a problem: as more funds chased the same statistical patterns, the patterns became less profitable, because the act of many funds trading on a pattern erodes the very inefficiency they're exploiting. This forced a relentless arms race, with quant firms hunting for ever more obscure relationships and investing heavily in speed to capture edges before competitors did.

That arms race produced a dramatic and instructive disaster in August 2007, an event known as the quant quake. For a few days that month, many of the largest and most successful quantitative funds suffered severe, simultaneous losses, and the strangest part was that nothing seemed to be happening in the broader market to explain it. What unfolded was a hidden chain reaction. Many quant funds, it turned out, were running similar statistical arbitrage strategies, holding similar positions based on similar models. When one large fund began selling, likely to reduce risk or meet demands for cash elsewhere, its selling pushed prices in ways that hurt the other funds holding the same positions. Those funds then faced losses and began selling too, which pushed prices further and inflicted more losses on everyone, a cascade of forced selling among funds that didn't even know how crowded their strategies had become. The models, all trained on similar data, had led different firms into the same trades, and when the unwinding started, they all suffered together. Within days, some of the most sophisticated funds in the world had lost enormous sums, only for many of the positions to recover shortly after as the forced selling exhausted itself. The quant quake revealed a hidden fragility: strategies that appear independent and diversified can be dangerously correlated when many players are running the same mathematics on the same data.

Factor Investing and Risk Premia

Factor investing rests on a discovery that reshaped how academics and practitioners think about returns: that the performance of stocks can be explained, to a large degree, by their exposure to a handful of common characteristics, and that some of these characteristics have reliably earned extra return over long periods. Understanding factors means understanding where stock returns actually come from, and it forms the intellectual backbone of a huge portion of quantitative investing.

The story begins with a simple question academics asked decades ago: why do some stocks earn higher returns than others? The first answer, from the 1960s, was that riskier stocks, those more sensitive to the overall market, earned more to compensate for that risk. This single-factor view, where market exposure explained returns, held for a while. Then researchers noticed it wasn't the whole story. Stocks seemed to earn extra returns based on other characteristics too, patterns the market-risk explanation couldn't account for. In the early 1990s, the economists Eugene Fama and Kenneth French published research showing that two additional characteristics, beyond market exposure, helped explain returns: company size and value. Their work opened the door to identifying a whole set of these return-driving characteristics, which came to be called factors.

A factor is a characteristic shared by many securities that's associated with a difference in returns. The main factors that decades of research have identified include several worth naming and understanding, because they represent distinct, persistent sources of return that quant funds try to capture systematically.

Factor	What It Captures	The Basic Idea
Value	Cheap stocks vs. expensive ones	Stocks trading cheaply relative to fundamentals tend to outperform over time

Size	Small companies vs. large ones	Smaller companies have historically earned higher returns than larger ones
Momentum	Recent winners vs. recent losers	Stocks that have risen recently tend to keep rising for a while
Quality	Profitable, stable firms vs. weak ones	Companies with strong, steady profitability tend to outperform
Low volatility	Calm stocks vs. wild ones	Less volatile stocks have earned surprisingly good risk-adjusted returns

Each of these factors represents a pattern that has persisted across many decades and many markets around the world, which is what gives investors confidence they're real rather than statistical flukes. The value factor, for instance, reflects the long-observed tendency of cheap stocks to outperform expensive ones over time, an idea that traces back to the foundational value investing of Benjamin Graham. Momentum captures the tendency of recent winners to keep winning, a pattern that seems to contradict value but coexists with it. Each factor tells a different story about why certain stocks earn more.

The deeper question is why these factors earn extra return at all, and there are two competing explanations that reflect a genuine divide in the field. The first explanation is that factors represent compensation for risk. Under this view, a factor earns extra return because it exposes the investor to some kind of danger, and the extra return is payment for bearing that danger. Value stocks, for example, might be cheap because they're genuinely riskier, companies in trouble or in declining industries, and the extra return compensates investors for taking on that risk. This is the risk premia interpretation: the factor return is a reward for accepting a specific risk that can't be diversified away.

The second explanation is that factors represent mistakes, persistent errors in how investors behave. Under this behavioral view, factors earn extra return because human psychology causes investors to systematically misprice certain stocks. Momentum might work because investors underreact to good news at first and then pile in later, creating a trend. Value might work because investors overreact to bad news, pushing troubled stocks too cheap. If factors come from behavioral mistakes rather than risk, they should persist as long as human psychology stays constant, which is to say more or less forever. The truth probably involves both explanations, with some factors reflecting real risk and others reflecting behavioral errors, and the debate between these interpretations remains unsettled.

The practical importance of factor research grew enormously when it revealed something uncomfortable about hedge fund returns. Researchers realized they could analyze a fund's performance and determine how much of it came from simple exposure to well-known factors, exposure any investor could get cheaply, versus how much came from genuine skill. This analysis was devastating for many funds. It turned out that a large portion of what some hedge funds called alpha, and charged enormous fees for, was actually just factor exposure dressed up as skill. A fund that loaded up on the value factor and the momentum factor might look like it was generating brilliant returns, when really it was just capturing well-documented factor premia that could be replicated for a fraction of the cost.

This realization gave rise to an entire industry built around cheap factor exposure. If factors drive returns and can be captured mechanically, why pay hedge fund fees to get them? Investment firms created products, often called smart beta funds, that systematically capture factor premia at low cost, offering investors exposure to value, momentum, quality, and other factors without the 2-and-20 fee structure. Asset managers like Dimensional Fund Advisors and AQR built large businesses on the insight that factors could be harvested systematically and cheaply, undercutting hedge funds that had been charging premium prices for what was, in part, just factor exposure. The rise of factor-based products pressured hedge funds to prove they were delivering something beyond factors, some genuine skill that couldn't be replicated by a cheap systematic strategy.

Machine Learning Applications in Portfolio Construction

The newest frontier in quantitative investing applies machine learning, the branch of artificial intelligence that lets computers find patterns in data without being explicitly programmed to look for them. Traditional quant models, like the factor and stat arb approaches described above, rely on humans specifying the relationships to exploit, a value factor, a mean-reverting pair. Machine learning flips this, letting the algorithm discover relationships on its own by searching through data for patterns that predict returns, including patterns no human would ever think to look for or could even articulate.

The distinction matters. In a traditional model, a researcher hypothesizes that some characteristic predicts returns, tests the hypothesis, and if it holds, builds a strategy around it. The human supplies the idea, and the computer verifies and executes it. In a machine learning model, the algorithm itself searches for whatever predicts returns, examining enormous quantities of data and identifying complex, subtle relationships that a human researcher might never hypothesize. The machine isn't told what to look for. It's told to find whatever works, and it can uncover intricate patterns involving many variables interacting in ways no person would design by hand.

The rise of machine learning in investing has been driven partly by an explosion in the data available to analyze, much of it unconventional. Beyond traditional financial data, quant funds now feed their models what's called alternative data, unconventional information sources that might contain predictive signals.

Alternative Data Type	What It Might Reveal
Satellite imagery of parking lots	How busy retail stores are, hinting at sales

Credit card transaction data	Consumer spending patterns in real time
Shipping and container traffic	Global trade flows and supply chain activity
Social media sentiment	Public mood toward companies or products
Web-scraping of prices and reviews	Demand and pricing trends before official reports
Satellite images of oil storage tanks	Global oil supply levels

These data sources illustrate how far quantitative investing has traveled from reading annual reports. A fund might analyze satellite photos of retailer parking lots to estimate how many customers are shopping, gaining an early read on sales before the company reports its earnings. It might track credit card data to see consumer spending shifting in real time, or count cargo containers at ports to gauge global trade. Machine learning models excel at finding patterns in these vast, messy, unconventional datasets, connecting a change in parking lot traffic to a likely move in a retailer's stock, for instance, in ways that would overwhelm human analysis.

Two Sigma and D.E. Shaw are among the firms that have pushed hardest into machine learning and data-driven investing, employing large teams of computer scientists and data experts to build models that learn from these enormous datasets. The approach has grown more sophisticated as computing power and data availability have expanded, and machine learning now influences a substantial and growing share of quantitative trading. The firms that master it can, in principle, find predictive signals invisible to everyone else, gaining an edge from patterns their competitors can't see.

But machine learning in investing carries a distinctive and serious danger, one that connects directly to the final topic of this chapter. Machine learning models are extraordinarily good at finding patterns, so good that they routinely find patterns that aren't real. A model turned loose on enough data will discover countless relationships that held in the past purely by chance and have no predictive power for the future. Because these models are so powerful and so complex, distinguishing the patterns that reflect something genuine from the patterns that are just noise becomes extremely difficult. A model might identify a relationship that looks stunningly predictive in historical data but is actually a coincidence, and betting real money on such a phantom pattern leads straight to losses. The very capability that makes machine learning attractive, its ability to find subtle patterns humans miss, is also what makes it dangerous, because it finds false patterns just as eagerly as real ones.

There's a further problem specific to the most complex machine learning models: they can become black boxes, systems whose decisions even their creators can't fully explain. When a model recommends a trade, the humans running it may not understand why, because the model's reasoning is buried in layers of mathematical complexity too intricate to interpret. This creates real discomfort. An investor handing money to a strategy nobody can explain is taking a particular kind of risk, trusting that the model has found something real when no one can articulate what that something is. Some firms deliberately favor simpler, more interpretable models for this reason, accepting slightly less predictive power in exchange for understanding what their models are actually doing and why.

Backtesting and Overfitting Risks

Every quantitative strategy is born from testing an idea against historical data, and this testing process contains the single greatest danger in all of quantitative investing. Understanding backtesting and its central pitfall, overfitting, is what separates quant investors who survive from those who blow up, and it deserves the most careful attention of anything in this chapter.

Backtesting means simulating how a strategy would have performed in the past by applying its rules to historical data. Before risking real money, a quant researcher tests her strategy against years or decades of historical prices to see whether it would have made money. If the strategy performs well in the backtest, generating strong returns with acceptable risk, it looks promising. If it performs poorly, it gets discarded. Backtesting seems like simple common sense: test your idea on the past before betting on the future. And used carefully, it's genuinely useful, letting researchers evaluate strategies without risking capital. The problem is that backtesting is extraordinarily easy to abuse, mostly without the researcher even realizing she's doing it.

The central danger is overfitting, and it's subtle enough that it deserves careful explanation. Overfitting happens when a strategy is tuned so precisely to historical data that it captures the random noise in that specific data rather than any genuine, repeatable pattern. Here's the trap. Any set of historical data contains real patterns and random noise mixed together. A strategy that's adjusted and refined until it perfectly fits the historical data ends up fitting both the real patterns and the noise. Because the noise was random and won't repeat, a strategy fitted to it will fail when applied to new data, even though it looked magnificent in the backtest. The strategy essentially memorized the past instead of learning something true about markets, and memorizing the past is worthless for predicting the future.

An analogy makes the danger concrete. Imagine a student who prepares for an exam by memorizing the answers to last year's specific test rather than learning the underlying subject. On last year's test, the student would score perfectly. But on this year's test, with different questions, the student fails completely, because memorizing specific answers taught nothing about the actual material. An overfitted trading strategy is exactly like that student. It has memorized the specific twists of historical data, which lets it score brilliantly on the past it memorized, but it fails on new data because it never learned anything genuinely predictive. The perfect backtest was an illusion created by fitting to noise.

Overfitting grows more dangerous the more a researcher tinkers with a strategy, and this is where good intentions lead to ruin. A researcher testing a strategy naturally wants to improve it. She adjusts a parameter, and the backtest improves. She adds a rule, and it improves further. She tweaks the timing, and it gets better still. Each adjustment makes the historical performance look better, so it feels like progress. But every one of these adjustments risks fitting the strategy more tightly to the noise in the historical data rather than to anything real. After enough tinkering, the researcher has produced a strategy with a spectacular backtest that's really just a monument to the random quirks of one particular dataset. The more she optimized, the worse the problem became, even as the backtest looked ever more impressive. This is why a beautiful backtest should inspire suspicion rather than confidence, a lesson that runs against every instinct.

A related trap is data mining, which is searching through enough data and enough possible strategies that you're guaranteed to find something that looks profitable by pure chance. If you test thousands of random strategies against historical data, some of them will show excellent returns purely by luck, the way that flipping enough coins guarantees some will come up heads many times in a row. A researcher who tests thousands of ideas and reports only the ones that worked has found nothing but statistical accidents dressed up as discoveries. The strategy that looked best among thousands tested is very likely the luckiest, not the best, and it will disappoint when traded with real money on forward market data.

The techniques quants use to guard against these dangers are worth understanding, because they represent hard-won discipline against a seductive trap.

Safeguard	How It Protects Against Overfitting
Out-of-sample testing	Test the strategy on data it wasn't built with, to see if it still works
Holding out data	Reserve a portion of history the researcher never looks at during development
Keeping models simple	Fewer rules and parameters mean less room to fit noise
Demanding an economic rationale	Require a real reason the strategy should work, not just that it did
Paper trading	Test the strategy live, without real money, before committing capital

The most important of these is out-of-sample testing, the practice of testing a strategy on data that wasn't used to build it. The idea is to develop the strategy on one portion of history and then test it on a completely separate portion the researcher never examined during development. If the strategy works on this fresh data it never saw, that's real evidence it captured something genuine rather than memorizing noise. If it works on the development data but fails on the fresh data, that's the signature of overfitting, proof the strategy learned nothing real. Rigorous quants hold out a portion of their data untouched, refusing even to look at it until the strategy is finalized, precisely so they have a clean test the strategy couldn't have been fitted to.

Demanding an economic rationale is another discipline that separates careful quants from reckless ones. Before trusting a strategy, a thoughtful researcher asks why it should work, what real feature of markets or human behavior would make this pattern persist into the future. If there's a sound reason, a behavioral tendency, a structural feature of how markets operate, the pattern is more likely to be real and to continue. If there's no explanation, if the strategy just happened to work in the backtest for reasons nobody can articulate, it's probably an accident that won't survive. Insisting on a genuine reason, rather than accepting a good backtest at face value, filters out many phantom patterns before they can cause damage.

The reason all of this matters so intensely is that overfitting has destroyed countless quantitative strategies and funds. The history of quantitative investing is littered with strategies that boasted magnificent backtests and then lost money the moment they traded real capital, because the backtests reflected fitted noise rather than durable patterns. A backtest can be made to look as good as the researcher wants through enough optimization, which means a backtest alone proves almost nothing. The genuine test is always the future, whether the strategy makes money on data that didn't exist when it was built.

This gap between a strategy's historical simulation and its real-world performance is the central challenge of quantitative investing, and respecting it, treating every gorgeous backtest with suspicion rather than excitement, is the mark of a quant who understands the difference between finding a real edge and fooling oneself.

Discussion Question

A quantitative strategy with a flawless backtest and a strategy that will actually make money in the future can look absolutely identical at the moment you decide whether to fund it, because the only difference between them, whether the pattern is real or fitted noise, can't be directly observed until real money has been at risk for a while. Given that the future is the only true test and the future hasn't happened yet, what would actually justify putting money behind a quant strategy at all, and how much of the confidence quants place in their models is genuine knowledge versus a more sophisticated version of the same overfitting they claim to guard against?

Chapter 7: Risk Management and Portfolio Construction

Most hedge funds that die don't die because their managers were bad at picking investments. They die because they couldn't survive being wrong. A manager can be right about ninety-five trades out of a hundred and still lose everything if the five losers were sized carelessly, funded with too much borrowed money, or held with a counterparty that failed at the worst moment. This is the uncomfortable truth that separates risk management from investing: making money is about being right, but staying alive is about what happens when you're wrong, and you will be wrong.

The strategies in the earlier chapters were all about generating returns, finding the good trade, the mispriced security, the closing merger. This chapter is about the other half of the job, the half that determines whether a fund survives long enough for its good ideas to pay off. Risk management isn't glamorous, and it rarely makes anyone rich on its own. What it does is prevent the single catastrophic event that erases years of careful work in an afternoon. The history of hedge funds is a graveyard of brilliant investors who understood markets deeply and failed anyway, because they neglected the unglamorous discipline of managing what could go wrong. We'll look at how funds measure their risk, how borrowed money amplifies both triumph and ruin, why the diversification that protects a portfolio can vanish exactly when it's needed, how much to bet on any single idea, and the hidden dangers that live in the relationships between a fund and the firms it depends on.

Value at Risk and Stress Testing

Before you can manage risk, you have to measure it, and the most widely used measurement in all of finance is Value at Risk, universally shortened to VaR. It attempts to answer a question every investor wants answered: how much could I lose? The answer VaR gives is precise, useful, and dangerously incomplete, and understanding both its power and its limits is the starting point for thinking clearly about risk.

Value at Risk expresses potential loss as a single number tied to a probability and a time period. A statement of VaR always has three parts: a confidence level, a time horizon, and a dollar amount. A fund might say its one-day VaR at 95 percent confidence is 10 million dollars. Translated into plain language, that means on 95 percent of days, the fund expects to lose no more than 10 million dollars, and on the remaining 5 percent of days, roughly one trading day in twenty, it expects to lose more than that. The number packages a complex distribution of possible outcomes into one digestible figure that a manager, an investor, or a regulator can grasp at a glance. That compression is why VaR became the standard risk measure used across banks, hedge funds, and regulators worldwide.

The appeal is obvious. A fund holding thousands of positions across dozens of markets needs some way to summarize its total risk in a form people can actually use, and VaR does exactly that. It lets a manager compare the risk of different portfolios, track how risk changes over time, and set limits, telling a trading desk it can't take positions that push VaR above a certain threshold. Regulators embraced it as a way to monitor whether financial institutions were taking on dangerous amounts of risk. For all these purposes, having a single, comparable number is genuinely helpful.

There are three main ways to calculate VaR, and each makes different assumptions that affect the answer.

Method	How It Works	Main Weakness
Historical	Uses actual past returns to estimate the range of losses	Assumes the future resembles the recent past
Parametric	Assumes returns follow a normal bell curve and calculates from its shape	The bell curve badly underestimates extreme events
Monte Carlo	Runs thousands of simulated random scenarios	Only as good as the assumptions fed into the simulation

The parametric method, in particular, harbors a flaw that has caused real disasters, and it's worth understanding because it reveals the deepest problem with VaR. The parametric approach assumes that returns follow a normal distribution, the familiar bell curve, in which extreme outcomes are vanishingly rare. Under a normal distribution, a market move of five or six standard deviations, a huge swing, should happen roughly once in the lifetime of the universe. The trouble is that financial markets don't actually follow a normal distribution. Real markets have what statisticians call fat tails, meaning extreme events happen far more often than the bell curve predicts. Market crashes, panics, and violent moves that the normal distribution says should almost never occur happen every few years. A model built on the bell curve systematically underestimates the likelihood and severity of exactly the events that destroy funds.

This failure showed itself vividly during the 2008 crisis. As markets convulsed, the head of finance at Goldman Sachs, David Viniar, remarked that the firm was seeing moves of 25 standard deviations, several days in a row. Under the normal distribution assumption baked into standard VaR models, a single 25-standard-deviation event shouldn't occur even once across a span of time vastly longer than the age of the universe, let alone several days running. The obvious conclusion wasn't that the firm had witnessed something cosmically impossible. It was that the models were wrong, that the bell curve had drastically understated how wild markets could get. The funds and banks that trusted their VaR numbers walked into 2008 believing they were far safer than they were, because the measurement told them extreme losses were nearly impossible right up until those losses arrived.

The most important limitation of VaR, though, is conceptual rather than computational, and it holds even for a perfectly calculated number. VaR tells you the threshold you'll exceed 5 percent of the time, but it tells you nothing about how bad things get once you cross that threshold. Return to the fund with a 10 million dollar VaR at 95 percent confidence. On the 5 percent of days when it loses more than 10 million, how much more does it lose? Eleven million? Fifty million? Everything? VaR is silent on this question. It defines the edge of the cliff but says nothing about how far the fall goes, and it's the depth of the fall, not the location of the edge, that actually kills a fund. A manager who obsesses over VaR can be lulled into false comfort, focusing on the 95 percent of normal days while remaining blind to the catastrophic 5 percent that determines survival.

The response to this blind spot is a related measure called Conditional Value at Risk, also known as Expected Shortfall. Where VaR asks what loss you'll exceed 5 percent of the time, Conditional VaR asks a better question: on those bad days when you do exceed the threshold, what's your average loss? It looks past the edge of the cliff and measures how far down the losses typically go. This makes it more informative about the extreme outcomes that matter most, and many sophisticated funds and regulators have shifted toward Expected Shortfall precisely because it captures the severity of tail events that plain VaR ignores. It's not a complete solution, since it still depends on modeling assumptions, but it directs attention to the part of the distribution where funds actually die.

Because every version of VaR relies on models and assumptions that can fail, serious risk management pairs it with stress testing, which abandons probability distributions entirely and simply asks what would happen under specific bad scenarios.

Rather than estimating a statistical range of losses, stress testing imagines a particular disaster and calculates the damage. What if the 2008 crisis happened again tomorrow? What if interest rates jumped two percentage points in a week? What if oil doubled, or a major currency collapsed, or a specific large position lost half its value overnight? Stress testing runs the portfolio through these hypothetical catastrophes to see how it would hold up.

Stress tests come in two broad types, and both matter. Historical scenarios replay actual past crises, applying the market moves from 2008, or the 1987 crash, or the 2020 pandemic shock, to the current portfolio to see what would happen if history repeated. Hypothetical scenarios imagine disasters that haven't occurred but plausibly could, a sudden war, a sovereign default, a liquidity freeze. A particularly useful variant is reverse stress testing, which flips the exercise around. Instead of asking how much a given scenario would cost, it asks what scenario would be severe enough to destroy the fund, working backward from catastrophe to identify the specific combination of events that would prove fatal. This forces a manager to confront her fund's deepest vulnerabilities directly rather than hoping they never surface.

The combination of VaR and stress testing reflects a mature understanding that no single measure captures risk adequately. VaR provides a useful everyday summary of normal risk, Expected Shortfall probes the severity of bad days, and stress testing examines specific catastrophes that models might miss. Together they form a more complete picture, though even the best risk measurement can't eliminate the fundamental problem: the future can always produce something no model anticipated, and the manager who forgets that, who mistakes a precise number for genuine safety, is the one most likely to be destroyed by it.

Leverage and Margin Requirements

Leverage is the use of borrowed money to increase the size of an investment, and it's the force that turns ordinary hedge fund losses into extinction events. Nearly every hedge fund that has collapsed spectacularly did so with the help of leverage, because leverage doesn't just amplify returns, it amplifies the speed and severity of losses in a way that can outrun a manager's ability to react. Understanding it fully is essential to understanding how funds die.

Start with what leverage does to returns. Suppose a fund has 100 million dollars of its own capital and borrows another 100 million, giving it 200 million to invest. Its leverage ratio is two to one, meaning its total positions are twice its actual capital. Now imagine its investments rise 10 percent. The 200 million grows to 220 million, a 20 million gain. But that gain is measured against the fund's own 100 million of capital, so the fund earned 20 percent on its capital from a 10 percent move in the market. Leverage doubled the return. This is why funds borrow: it magnifies gains, turning modest market moves into impressive returns on the capital investors actually put up.

The problem is that leverage is perfectly symmetrical, and the downside is where it becomes lethal. Take the same leveraged fund and suppose its investments fall 10 percent instead of rising. The 200 million drops to 180 million, a 20 million loss, which against the fund's 100 million of capital is a 20 percent loss. The same borrowing that doubled the gain now doubles the loss. Push the leverage higher and the effect grows more violent. A fund levered ten to one, with 100 million of capital controlling a billion dollars of positions, would be wiped out entirely by a mere 10 percent decline in its investments, because a 10 percent loss on a billion dollars is 100 million, the fund's entire capital. The higher the leverage, the smaller the market move needed to destroy the fund.

Here's how the same 10 percent market move plays out at different levels of leverage, which makes the danger unmistakable.

Leverage Ratio	Capital	Total Position	Effect of a 10% Market Gain	Effect of a 10% Market Loss
1 to 1 (none)	$100M	$100M	+10% on capital	-10% on capital
2 to 1	$100M	$200M	+20% on capital	-20% on capital

5 to 1	$100M	$500M	+50% on capital	-50% on capital
10 to 1	$100M	$1,000M	+100% on capital	-100%, wiped out
25 to 1	$100M	$2,500M	+250% on capital	Destroyed by a 4% loss

Look at the bottom row. A fund levered 25 to one is destroyed by a market move of just 4 percent against it, a decline so small it happens routinely. This isn't a hypothetical extreme. It describes an actual fund that stands as the most instructive disaster in hedge fund history.

Long-Term Capital Management was founded in 1994 by John Meriwether, a legendary bond trader, and its roster included two economists, Myron Scholes and Robert Merton, who would win the Nobel Prize in economics in 1997 for their work on pricing options. The firm was, by reputation and by credentials, the smartest collection of financial minds ever assembled in one place. Its strategy involved finding tiny pricing discrepancies between related bonds and betting they would converge, the kind of relative value trades where the profit on any single trade is minuscule.

To turn those tiny edges into large returns, LTCM used enormous leverage. At its peak, the firm had borrowed roughly 25 dollars for every dollar of its own capital, and when derivatives were included, its effective leverage was far higher still, by some estimates exceeding 100 to one. The firm controlled positions of well over a trillion dollars in notional value on a capital base of a few billion.

For its first years, the strategy worked beautifully, delivering returns above 40 percent as the tiny discrepancies converged just as the models predicted. Then in 1998, Russia defaulted on its government debt, an event the models treated as nearly impossible. The default triggered a global panic, and investors fled from exactly the kinds of positions LTCM held, causing the price relationships the firm had bet on to diverge violently instead of converging. Because LTCM was levered so extraordinarily, even modest adverse moves inflicted staggering losses. Their own models had ignored how correlations and risk could be affected due to their own presence in the markets they traded. Within weeks, the firm lost most of its capital. Its positions were so large that the Federal Reserve, fearing LTCM's collapse would drag down the entire financial system, organized a rescue in which a group of major banks injected capital to unwind the fund in an orderly way. The smartest people in finance, armed with Nobel Prize-winning models, had been destroyed not because their analysis was wrong in the long run, many of their trades would eventually have converged as predicted, but because their leverage was so extreme they couldn't survive the short-run losses long enough to be proven right. The lesson burned into the industry: leverage doesn't just magnify outcomes, it removes your ability to endure being temporarily wrong, and being temporarily wrong is guaranteed.

The mechanism that makes leverage so dangerous in a crisis is the margin call, and understanding it explains why leveraged losses accelerate rather than unfold gently.

When a fund borrows to invest, it must post collateral, called margin, with its lender, essentially a deposit that protects the lender if the fund's positions lose money. As long as the positions hold their value, everything is fine. But when the positions fall, the collateral no longer covers the lender's risk, so the lender issues a margin call, demanding the fund post more collateral immediately. The fund must come up with cash fast, and if it doesn't have spare cash lying around, it has to sell positions to raise it. Here's where the trap springs shut. The fund is forced to sell into a falling market, at the worst possible prices, which locks in losses and often pushes prices down further, triggering more margin calls, forcing more selling, in a self-reinforcing spiral. A leveraged fund in a falling market can be forced to liquidate everything at fire-sale prices, not because its investments were fundamentally worthless, but because it ran out of collateral and had no choice. This forced-selling spiral is how leverage converts a temporary decline into permanent destruction.

Leverage also comes in forms less obvious than straightforward borrowing, and the hidden kinds are often the most dangerous because they obscure how much risk a fund is really taking. Beyond borrowing cash outright, a fund can gain leverage through derivatives, which let it control a large position while putting up only a small amount of money. It can use repurchase agreements, called repo, to borrow against securities it owns. It can use total return swaps, contracts that give it the economic exposure of owning an asset without actually buying it, and therefore without the borrowing showing up plainly on its books. These embedded forms of leverage can hide a fund's true risk from lenders, investors, and even from the fund itself, because the leverage isn't a simple loan anyone can see. As a later section shows, this kind of hidden leverage through swaps produced one of the largest and most sudden hedge fund collapses in recent history.

Correlation Breakdown in Market Crises

The entire logic of diversification rests on a single assumption, and that assumption fails at precisely the moment diversification matters most. This is one of the cruelest features of financial markets, and understanding it separates investors who merely believe in diversification from those who understand its limits.

Diversification works because different investments don't move in perfect lockstep. If you own a range of assets that behave differently from one another, the ones that fall on a given day are offset by the ones that rise, so your overall portfolio is steadier than any single holding. The mathematical measure of how closely two assets move together is correlation, ranging from perfect positive correlation, where they move identically, to zero correlation, where their movements are unrelated, to negative correlation, where one rises when the other falls. A well-diversified portfolio combines assets with low correlations to one another, so their independent movements smooth out the whole. This is the foundation of nearly all serious portfolio construction, and in normal times it works.

The problem is that correlations aren't fixed. They shift with market conditions, and specifically, they tend to spike toward one during crises. Assets that normally move independently suddenly all fall together when panic strikes, which means the diversification that protected the portfolio in calm times evaporates exactly when protection is needed most. An investor who carefully spread money across many uncorrelated assets can watch, in horror, as every one of them drops simultaneously during a market crash, the careful diversification providing no shelter at all. The correlations that appeared in the historical data, that justified the whole portfolio construction, break down under stress.

Here's a simplified picture of how correlations shift between normal times and a crisis, which shows why diversification fails when it does.

Asset Pair	Correlation in Normal Times	Correlation in a Crisis
US stocks and European stocks	Moderate	Very high, both crash together
Stocks and corporate bonds	Low	High, both fall as panic spreads
Different hedge fund strategies	Low, they seem independent	High, forced selling links them
Emerging markets and developed markets	Moderate	Very high, capital flees everything risky

The reason correlations spike in crises comes down to human behavior and the mechanics of forced selling. When panic sets in, investors stop distinguishing between assets based on their individual merits and instead sell whatever they can to raise cash and reduce risk. This indiscriminate selling drives everything down together, regardless of the fundamental relationships between the assets. Leveraged investors facing margin calls are forced to sell across their entire portfolios at once, dumping good and bad positions alike, which links assets that had nothing to do with one another. A flight to quality sends everyone rushing into the safest assets, like government bonds, while selling everything else simultaneously. The result is that in a genuine crisis, almost everything risky falls together, and the only things that rise are the handful of true safe havens. Correlation, in the moments that matter, marches toward one.

Long-Term Capital Management, again, illustrates this perfectly. The firm believed its positions were diversified because it held many different trades across different markets and different countries, trades that appeared, in the historical data, to be largely independent of one another. The models said that even if a few trades went wrong, the others would hold up, so the diversified portfolio was safe. But in the 1998 panic, every one of those supposedly independent trades moved against the firm at the same time, because they all shared a hidden common thread: they were all bets that depended on markets remaining calm and price relationships behaving normally. When panic replaced calm everywhere at once, the diversification that existed on paper vanished, and the losses hit every position simultaneously. What looked like many independent bets turned out to be, underneath, a single concentrated bet on market stability, and when that one bet failed, everything failed together.

The lesson threads through everything in this chapter and connects back to the diversification discussed in earlier chapters. Correlations measured in calm markets are not reliable guides to how assets will behave in a crisis. A portfolio that appears well-diversified based on normal-times correlations may be far more concentrated than it looks, if all its holdings secretly depend on some common condition, market calm, easy borrowing, continued economic growth, that will fail all at once when a crisis hits. Genuine risk management requires looking past the comfortable correlations of good times and asking what would happen if those relationships broke down together, because in the worst moments, they will.

Position Sizing and Concentration Limits

Deciding how much to invest in any single position is one of the most consequential choices a manager makes, and it's a separate skill from deciding what to invest in. A manager can identify a wonderful opportunity and still ruin herself by betting too much on it, because a position sized too large can inflict a fatal loss if that one idea, however brilliant it seemed, turns out wrong. Position sizing is the discipline of controlling how much any single bet can hurt you.

The core tension is between conviction and survival. A manager who's confident in an idea wants to bet heavily on it, because a large position on a winning idea produces large profits. But a large position on a losing idea produces large losses, and no idea is ever certain. The art of position sizing is balancing the desire to profit from good ideas against the need to survive bad ones, ensuring that no single position, no matter how compelling, can do catastrophic damage if it fails. This means even a manager's highest-conviction idea should usually be capped at a size the fund could absorb losing, because the one thing a manager can never afford is a single bet large enough to end the fund.

One formal approach to this problem is the Kelly criterion, a mathematical formula that calculates the optimal bet size based on the edge you have and the odds you face. The formula, developed originally for gambling, tells you the fraction of your capital to wager to maximize long-term growth, given your probability of winning and the payoff. Its main lesson is that bet size should scale with your edge: the bigger and more certain your advantage, the more you should bet, but even substantial edges call for betting only a fraction of your capital, never everything. In practice, many investors use a fraction of what the Kelly formula suggests, called fractional Kelly, because the full Kelly bet is uncomfortably aggressive and vulnerable to any error in estimating your true edge. The broader idea stands: rational bet sizing is proportional to your advantage and always leaves room to survive being wrong.

Beyond sizing individual positions, funds impose concentration limits, rules capping how much of the portfolio can be exposed to any single position, sector, or theme. These limits enforce diversification by preventing the portfolio from becoming too dependent on any one thing. A fund might limit any single position to a small percentage of its capital, cap its exposure to any one industry, and restrict how much can be tied to any single risk factor or theme. The purpose is to ensure that no single adverse event, a collapse in one stock, one sector, one type of bet, can inflict damage the fund can't survive. Concentration limits are a way of institutionalizing humility, of admitting in advance that any individual conviction might be wrong and building the portfolio so that being wrong about one thing isn't fatal.

The danger of ignoring concentration limits was demonstrated by Amaranth Advisors, a hedge fund that collapsed in 2006 in one of the fastest large blowups ever. A single trader at the firm, Brian Hunter, made enormous bets on natural gas prices, wagering that the relationship between gas prices in different months would move a particular way. The positions grew so large that Amaranth effectively controlled a huge share of the natural gas futures market, a concentration far beyond any prudent limit. When natural gas prices moved sharply against Hunter's bets, the concentrated positions produced catastrophic losses. Amaranth lost roughly 6 billion dollars in a matter of weeks, most of it from that single concentrated natural gas bet, and the fund collapsed. Had the firm enforced sensible concentration limits, capping how much it would risk on any single trade or market, the losses would have been painful but survivable. Instead, the concentration turned a bad bet into an extinction event. The episode is a stark reminder that concentration magnifies both the reward when you're right and the destruction when you're wrong, and that even a talented trader with a plausible thesis can destroy a fund by betting too much on a single idea.

Counterparty and Prime Brokerage Risk

The final category of risk isn't about the fund's investments being wrong. It's about the firms the fund depends on failing, and it's a danger many managers overlook until it materializes. A hedge fund doesn't operate in isolation. It relies on a web of relationships with banks, brokers, and trading partners, and if one of those partners fails, the fund can suffer devastating losses even if every one of its own investment decisions was sound. This is counterparty risk, the risk that the other side of your dealings collapses.

At the center of a hedge fund's operations sits its prime broker, usually a large investment bank that provides the fund with a bundle of essential services. The prime broker lends the fund money and securities, enabling its borrowing and short selling. It holds the fund's assets in custody. It clears and settles the fund's trades. It provides the financing that lets the fund operate at scale. A hedge fund is deeply dependent on its prime broker for the basic machinery of doing business, which means the health of the prime broker directly affects the safety of the fund. If the prime broker runs into trouble, the fund's assets and operations can be caught in the wreckage.

The catastrophic version of this risk arrived when Lehman Brothers collapsed in September 2008. Lehman was a major prime broker, holding the assets of many hedge funds, particularly through its London operation. When Lehman filed for bankruptcy, hedge funds that had their assets held at Lehman's prime brokerage discovered those assets were frozen, tangled up in the bankruptcy proceedings, and inaccessible for months or years. The funds hadn't made any investment mistake. Their positions might have been perfectly sound. But because their prime broker failed, their assets were trapped, and some funds were crippled or destroyed simply because they'd entrusted their holdings to a firm that went under. The mechanism that made this so damaging involved a practice called rehypothecation, in which the prime broker was permitted to reuse the fund's collateral for its own purposes. When Lehman collapsed, assets that funds thought were safely theirs had been rehypothecated into Lehman's own dealings and became entangled in the bankruptcy, far harder to recover than the funds had ever imagined.

The lesson from Lehman reshaped how hedge funds think about counterparty risk. Before 2008, many funds concentrated all their business with a single prime broker for convenience, never seriously contemplating that a major investment bank could actually fail. Afterward, funds spread their business across multiple prime brokers, so that the failure of any one wouldn't trap all their assets, and they scrutinized the financial health of their brokers far more carefully. The comfortable assumption that a large bank was permanently safe had been shattered, and managing the risk of a counterparty's collapse became a permanent part of running a fund.

Counterparty risk resurfaced dramatically in 2021 with the collapse of Archegos Capital Management, which combined hidden leverage and counterparty risk into a single spectacular failure that inflicted enormous losses on the banks involved. Archegos, run by Bill Hwang, was technically a family office rather than a traditional hedge fund, but its downfall illustrates counterparty and leverage risk with brutal clarity. Hwang built enormous concentrated positions in a handful of stocks, but he did so largely through total return swaps, the derivative contracts that gave him the economic exposure of owning the stocks without actually holding them in his own name. Because he used swaps arranged separately with several different banks, no single bank could see the full scale of his positions. Each prime broker knew only its own slice of his exposure, not the total, so each extended him leverage based on an incomplete picture, unaware that other banks were doing the same thing simultaneously.

The result was that Archegos accumulated staggering leverage across multiple banks, none of which understood the true magnitude of what they'd enabled. When the stocks Hwang had concentrated in began to fall in March 2021, the swaps generated massive losses, and the banks issued margin calls Archegos couldn't meet. As Archegos defaulted, the banks rushed to sell the underlying stocks to limit their losses, and the forced selling drove the stocks down further, deepening everyone's losses in a familiar spiral. The banks that had served as Archegos's counterparties absorbed the damage. Credit Suisse lost roughly 5.5 billion dollars, a blow that contributed to the bank's later troubles, and Nomura lost billions more. Archegos itself was wiped out, but the more startling part was how much it cost the banks that had extended it leverage without grasping their true exposure.

Here's how the losses from the Archegos collapse fell across its counterparties, which shows how one fund's failure became many firms' problem.

Bank	Approximate Loss	Why

Credit Suisse	~$5.5 billion	Large swap exposure, slow to unwind positions
Nomura	~$2.9 billion	Significant exposure to Archegos swaps
Morgan Stanley	~$900 million	Exposure partly reduced by selling faster
Various others	Smaller amounts	Moved quickly to exit positions

The Archegos episode carried lessons in several directions at once. For the banks, it exposed the danger of extending leverage to a client without understanding its total exposure across the market, and the peril of the hidden leverage that swaps make possible. For anyone studying risk, it reinforced how counterparty risk runs in both directions: a fund can be endangered by its counterparties failing, and counterparties can be endangered by a fund failing. The web of relationships that lets hedge funds operate also transmits risk between them, so that one participant's collapse can inflict losses on everyone connected to it. Managing counterparty risk means understanding not just your own positions but the health and exposure of everyone you deal with, because in a crisis, the failure of a partner can hurt you as badly as any mistake of your own.

Discussion Question

Long-Term Capital Management was run by Nobel Prize winners whose trades would mostly have been proven right if they'd survived long enough, yet they were destroyed because their leverage left them no room to endure being temporarily wrong. This suggests that surviving in markets depends less on being right than on structuring your risk so that being wrong can't kill you. But excessive caution has its own cost: a manager who takes too little risk, uses no leverage, and caps every position tightly will produce returns so modest that investors won't pay for them, and the fund dies a slower death from irrelevance. Where's the line between the discipline that keeps a fund alive and the caution that makes it pointless, and is it even possible to know which side of that line you're on until after the crisis that tests it?

Chapter 8: Due Diligence and Manager Selection

Here's a fact that should unsettle anyone about to hand money to a hedge fund. The single most impressive thing about a manager, the smooth and steadily rising track record that makes investors feel safe, is often the very thing that should make them suspicious. Bernie Madoff produced returns so consistent, so free of the ups and downs that plague real investing, that thousands of sophisticated investors concluded he must be a genius. He was running the largest Ponzi scheme in history. The returns were fabricated, and their impossible smoothness was the tell, if anyone had known how to read it.

Choosing a manager is where most investors in this field make their biggest mistakes, and the mistakes are rarely about picking a manager whose strategy underperforms. They're about picking a manager who turns out to be a fraud, whose operations were a house of cards, whose track record was an illusion, or whose interests were quietly opposed to the investor's own. The work of investigating a manager before investing is called due diligence, and it's a discipline in its own right, separate from and arguably more important than analyzing whether a strategy is any good. A brilliant strategy run by a dishonest or careless manager will destroy your capital just as surely as a bad strategy.

Here we cover how serious investors examine the people they're considering trusting, from the deceptions hidden in track records, to the operational failures that sink funds, to the terms that reveal whose side a manager is really on, to the background checks that catch what everything else misses.

Evaluating Track Records and Survivorship Bias

A track record is the first thing any investor looks at, and it's also the most misleading document a manager will ever show you. The numbers feel like hard evidence, a factual history of what the manager achieved, and investors instinctively treat a strong track record as proof of skill. But track records are riddled with distortions, some accidental and some deliberate, and learning to see through them is the foundation of manager evaluation.

Start with the deepest distortion, one that infects nearly every comparison investors make: survivorship bias. When people evaluate hedge funds, they look at the funds that exist today and their historical returns. The problem is that the funds existing today are the survivors. The funds that performed badly, lost money, and shut down have vanished from view, taking their poor returns with them. So when you look at the track records of currently operating funds, or at industry averages compiled from surviving funds, you're seeing only the winners, because the losers already disappeared. This makes the whole industry look far more successful than it ever actually was.

The effect is enormous and easy to underestimate. Imagine a thousand funds launch. Over the next decade, the four hundred that performed worst shut down, one by one, as investors flee and managers give up. Ten years later, someone studies the six hundred surviving funds and finds they averaged healthy returns. But that average is a fiction, because it excludes the four hundred failures that dragged down the true picture. The real average across all thousand funds, including the dead ones, was far lower. Survivorship bias means that published hedge fund returns, industry indices, and casual comparisons systematically overstate how well funds actually do, because the dead are silent and only the living report their numbers.

There's a second, related distortion that inflates track records even further, called backfill bias or instant history bias. When a new fund launches, it typically doesn't report its returns to the databases that track the industry right away. It waits. It reports to a database only once it has a good record to show, and when it finally joins, it backfills its entire history into the database, including those strong early returns. The funds that launched and stumbled never join the database at all, because they have nothing attractive to report. The result is that the databases are stuffed with impressive early track records that were added retroactively by funds that had already succeeded, while the funds that failed early are absent entirely. This makes reported industry returns look even better than survivorship bias alone would suggest.

Here are the main distortions that corrupt track records, each of which pushes reported performance higher than reality.

Bias	How It Works	Effect on Reported Returns
Survivorship	Failed funds disappear from the data	Inflates averages by hiding the losers
Backfill	Funds report only after they have good early returns	Adds strong histories that exclude early failures
Selection	Managers show only their best funds or periods	Presents a flattering, unrepresentative slice
Smoothing	Illiquid holdings priced infrequently look calmer	Understates true volatility and risk

Beyond these structural biases lies a more basic question that investors routinely fail to ask: how long a track record do you actually need before it means anything? The intuitive answer, that a few years of strong returns proves skill, is badly wrong. Distinguishing genuine skill from luck requires a great deal of data, far more than most track records provide. A manager who produces three years of excellent returns might be highly skilled, or might simply be one of the many managers who got lucky, the way that among thousands of coin-flippers, some will produce long streaks of heads by chance alone. With a short track record, there's no statistical way to tell the skilled manager from the lucky one, because both look identical over a brief span. Genuine confidence that returns reflect skill rather than luck often requires a decade or more of data, and even then it's not certain.

This connects to a body of research that investors find inconvenient: hedge fund performance persistence is weak. Studies examining whether past winners continue to win in the future have generally found that strong past performance is a poor predictor of strong future performance. The managers who topped the rankings in one period frequently drift toward the middle or the bottom in the next, and yesterday's stars are often tomorrow's disappointments.

This finding cuts against the entire instinct to chase managers with the best recent records, because that record, however impressive, tells you surprisingly little about what comes next. Investors who pile into last year's best-performing fund are frequently buying in right before the performance reverts.

Even when a track record is real and long, the more important question is how the returns were generated, because the source of past returns determines whether they can continue. A manager might have produced wonderful returns simply by riding a rising market, in which case the returns reflect market exposure anyone could have gotten cheaply, not skill. Or the returns might have come from loading up on well-known factors, as discussed earlier, dressed up as manager brilliance. Or they might have come from taking enormous hidden risks that happened not to blow up yet, the kind of strategy that produces steady gains for years and then a catastrophic loss. Understanding the source, whether returns came from genuine skill, from market exposure, from factor bets, or from uncompensated risk-taking, matters far more than the returns themselves, because only genuine skill is likely to persist.

The Sharpe ratio, the measure of return per unit of risk introduced earlier, is the standard tool investors use to judge track records, and it too can deceive. A high Sharpe ratio, indicating strong returns with low volatility, looks like the signature of a skilled, careful manager. But the Sharpe ratio can be manipulated, particularly by funds holding illiquid assets that get priced infrequently. When assets are marked to market rarely, or valued by the manager's own estimates rather than by real market prices, their apparent volatility is artificially low, because the price simply doesn't move between valuations even though the underlying value is fluctuating. This makes the fund look far less risky than it is, producing a flattering Sharpe ratio that reflects the infrequent pricing rather than genuine stability. A suspiciously smooth return stream, with a Sharpe ratio too good to be true, should prompt hard questions about how the fund values its holdings.

Which returns us to Madoff, whose track record was the perfect illustration of smoothness as a warning sign. Madoff reported returns of roughly ten to twelve percent a year, positive almost every single month, for decades, with almost none of the volatility that real investing produces. To naive investors, this consistency was the proof of his genius, evidence that he had found some reliable edge. To anyone who understood markets, the consistency was impossible. No legitimate strategy produces steady positive returns month after month for years without meaningful losing periods, because markets don't cooperate that way. The very smoothness that attracted investors was the mathematical fingerprint of fabrication. Harry Markopolos, a financial analyst, recognized this and spent years trying to warn regulators that Madoff's returns couldn't be real, running the numbers and concluding that no honest strategy could produce them. He was largely ignored until the scheme collapsed in 2008. The lesson is permanent: returns that look too consistent, too smooth, too good to be true, deserve suspicion rather than admiration, because reality is messier than fraud.

Operational Due Diligence Checklist

Investors naturally focus on a manager's investment ability, whether she can pick good trades, and neglect a category of risk that actually causes more fund failures: operational risk. Operational due diligence, often shortened to ODD, examines everything about a fund other than its investment strategy, the plumbing, the controls, the service providers, the handling of money, and it's where many of the worst disasters are caught, or missed. Studies of hedge fund failures have found that a large share, by some estimates around half, stemmed not from bad investing but from operational problems: fraud, mismanagement, poor controls, and outright theft. A fund can have a superb strategy and still be a catastrophe waiting to happen if its operations are rotten.

The most important operational principle is separation of duties, the idea that the manager who invests the money should not also be the one who holds it, values it, and reports on it. In a properly run fund, several independent parties each handle a different function, so that no single party can fabricate results or steal assets without others detecting it. The manager makes investment decisions, but independent firms hold the assets, calculate the fund's value, and audit the books. This separation is the structural defense against fraud, because it means the manager can't simply invent numbers or quietly divert money. When one party controls everything, that defense collapses, and the door to fraud swings open.

Here are the essential service providers a legitimate fund uses, and what each one does to protect investors.

Service Provider	Role	Why It Protects You
Independent administrator	Calculates the fund's value and holdings independently	The manager can't fabricate returns or asset values
Reputable auditor	Audits the fund's financial statements each year	An outside firm verifies the books are real
Custodian / prime broker	Holds the fund's assets separately from the manager	The manager can't simply take the money

Legal counsel	Structures the fund and reviews compliance	Ensures the fund follows the rules

The independent administrator deserves particular attention, because it performs the function most central to preventing fraud: calculating the fund's net asset value, its actual worth, independently of the manager. When an outside administrator prices the portfolio and computes returns, investors receive numbers verified by a party with no incentive to lie. When a manager self-administers, calculating and reporting her own returns without independent verification, investors are simply trusting the manager's word, with nothing to confirm it. Self-administration is one of the brightest red flags in all of due diligence, because it removes the single most important check on fraud.

Madoff, once again, is the case study, because his operation violated nearly every one of these principles at once, and the violations were visible to anyone who looked. He self-custodied assets, meaning the money was held within his own firm rather than at an independent custodian, so there was nothing stopping him from spending it. He effectively self-administered, generating his own account statements rather than having an independent administrator verify them. And his auditor, the firm responsible for confirming that his billions of dollars in reported assets were real, was a tiny, obscure accounting shop called Friehling & Horowitz, operating out of a small strip-mall office with three employees, one of whom was in his seventies and living in Florida, and one of whom was a secretary. A multibillion-dollar investment operation audited by a three-person storefront firm nobody had heard of was an absurdity that should have ended any investor's interest immediately. The auditor wasn't auditing anything; it was a rubber stamp.

Here are the operational red flags that Madoff's operation displayed, each of which should stop a diligent investor cold.

Red Flag	What Madoff Did	What It Should Have Signaled
Self-custody of assets	Held client money within his own firm	The manager can spend or divert the money
No independent administrator	Generated his own account statements	The reported returns can't be verified
Tiny, unknown auditor	Used a three-person storefront firm	The financials aren't being genuinely audited
Family in control roles	Relatives held compliance and key positions	No independent check on the principal

Secrecy about strategy	Refused to explain how he made returns	Something is being hidden

The tragedy is that these red flags weren't subtle or hidden. They were available to any investor or advisor who performed basic operational due diligence, asking who holds the assets, who calculates the returns, and who audits the books. The investors who did this work, and some did, refused to invest with Madoff precisely because the operational structure made no sense. The investors who lost everything were those who focused entirely on the attractive returns and never examined the plumbing beneath them. Operational due diligence isn't glamorous, and it feels like paperwork next to the excitement of a great track record, but it's exactly the work that separates the investors who avoided Madoff from those who were ruined by him.

Beyond fraud prevention, operational due diligence examines a range of practical matters that determine whether a fund can function reliably. Valuation policies matter enormously, especially for funds holding hard-to-price assets: who decides what those assets are worth, and how independent is that process? A fund that lets the manager value her own illiquid holdings, with no outside check, invites both honest error and dishonest manipulation. Business continuity planning matters: what happens if the office burns down, the systems fail, or a disaster strikes? Cybersecurity has grown into a real concern, since funds hold sensitive financial data and move large sums electronically. Key person risk, the danger that the fund depends entirely on one irreplaceable individual, needs assessment: what happens to the fund if the founder dies, falls ill, or leaves? And regulatory and compliance history reveals whether the manager has run afoul of the rules before. Each of these operational dimensions can determine whether a fund survives, independent of how good its investments are.

Assessing Fund Terms and Alignment of Interests

The terms of a fund, the fees, the liquidity provisions, the legal fine print, aren't just administrative details. They reveal whose interests the fund is built to serve, and reading them carefully tells you whether the manager's incentives point in the same direction as yours or the opposite. The central question running through all of it is alignment: does the manager win when you win, and lose when you lose, or has she arranged things so she profits regardless of how you fare?

The most powerful alignment mechanism is simple and worth prioritizing above almost everything else: how much of the manager's own money is invested in the fund. When a manager has a large portion of her personal wealth in the same fund, on the same terms as outside investors, her interests genuinely match theirs, because she suffers the same losses and enjoys the same gains. This is often called skin in the game, and it's the single most reliable sign that a manager's incentives are aligned with her investors. A manager with substantial personal capital at risk will manage that capital carefully, because it's her own money on the line, not just other people's. A manager with little or none of her own money in the fund faces a different calculus: she collects fees regardless, and the downside of losses falls entirely on investors while she keeps her management fee. When evaluating a fund, one of the first questions to ask is how much the manager has personally invested, because a large personal commitment does more to align interests than any contractual term.

Fee structures, examined earlier in this book, deserve scrutiny during due diligence not just for their size but for what they reveal about alignment. The performance fee, the manager's share of profits, aligns interests by paying the manager more when investors earn more.

But the details matter. Does the fund have a high-water mark, ensuring the manager only earns performance fees on genuine new gains rather than on recovering prior losses? Without one, a manager can lose investors' money, then charge performance fees again as she merely climbs back to where she started, which misaligns interests badly. Is there a hurdle rate, so the manager earns performance fees only on returns above what investors could have earned safely? The presence or absence of these features shifts the balance of interests between manager and investor, and a fund lacking a high-water mark should raise immediate concern.

Liquidity terms carry a danger that's easy to overlook: the mismatch between how easily investors can withdraw and how easily the fund can actually sell its holdings. A well-structured fund matches its redemption terms to the liquidity of its underlying investments. A fund holding easily sold, liquid assets can safely offer investors frequent redemptions, because it can raise cash quickly to meet withdrawals. But a fund holding illiquid assets that take months or years to sell must impose long lock-ups and infrequent redemptions, because it can't quickly turn its holdings into cash. The danger arises when a fund offers generous liquidity to investors while holding illiquid assets, a mismatch that looks attractive but is structurally unstable. If many investors try to withdraw at once, such a fund can't sell its illiquid holdings fast enough to pay them, and it's forced either to gate redemptions, trapping investors, or to dump its holdings at fire-sale prices, harming everyone. A liquidity mismatch between what the fund promises investors and what its assets can actually deliver is a hidden fragility that surfaces at the worst possible time.

Here's how favorable and unfavorable fund terms compare across the dimensions that matter most for alignment.

Term	Investor-Friendly	Investor-Unfriendly
Manager's own capital	Large personal investment in the fund	Little or none of the manager's money
High-water mark	Present, manager earns fees only on new gains	Absent, manager can charge twice for the same gains
Hurdle rate	Present, fees only on returns above a threshold	Absent, fees from the first dollar

Liquidity match	Redemption terms match the assets' liquidity	Generous liquidity on illiquid holdings
Transparency	Regular, detailed reporting to investors	Vague, infrequent, secretive reporting
Governance	Independent directors overseeing the fund	Manager controls everything, no oversight

Transparency and governance round out the assessment of terms. A fund that reports regularly and in detail, giving investors a genuine view of what it holds and how it's performing, treats its investors as partners entitled to understand their investment. A fund that reveals little, reports vaguely, and resists questions is either hiding something or treating investors with a disregard that should worry them. Fund governance matters too: does the fund have independent directors who oversee the manager and represent investors' interests, or does the manager control every aspect with no outside oversight? Independent governance provides a check on the manager, someone with a duty to investors who can raise concerns and demand answers. A fund where the manager answers to no one carries more risk that her interests will diverge from investors' without anyone noticing until it's too late.

Reference Checks and Background Verification

The final piece of due diligence addresses something the numbers and documents can't reveal: the character and history of the people running the fund. A track record shows what a manager did with money, and operational review shows how the fund is structured, but neither tells you whether the manager is honest, competent, and who she claims to be. Reference checks and background verification investigate the human beings behind the fund, and they catch problems that every other form of analysis misses.

Reference checks mean talking to people who know the manager, current and former investors, former employers, colleagues, business partners, to build a picture of her reputation, competence, and integrity. What people say about a manager, particularly those who have worked closely with her or entrusted her with money before, reveals things no document captures. Did former investors have good experiences, or did they leave frustrated and distrustful? Do former colleagues respect her, or do they describe problems with her judgment or ethics? These conversations surface the reputation and character that determine whether a manager can be trusted, information that exists only in the memories of people who have dealt with her.

The discipline that separates serious reference checking from a superficial version is the use of off-list references. A manager will happily provide a list of references, and those references will invariably say wonderful things, because the manager selected them precisely for that reason. The people on a manager's own reference list are the ones she knows will praise her. Genuine reference checking goes beyond this curated list to find people the manager didn't suggest, former employees who left on bad terms, investors who withdrew their money, competitors and colleagues who can speak candidly without having been pre-selected to flatter. These off-list references, the ones the manager didn't choose and might prefer you never spoke to, often provide the most honest and useful picture, precisely because they weren't hand-picked to deliver a favorable verdict.

Background verification is the more formal side, checking the factual claims and history that a manager presents. This includes verifying regulatory history through the records regulators maintain, which document any disciplinary actions, sanctions, or complaints against a manager or firm. It includes checking for litigation, lawsuits that might reveal disputes, misconduct, or financial trouble. It includes criminal background checks, and, importantly, verifying the manager's stated credentials and employment history, because people lie on resumes more often than investors assume. A manager who claims degrees she never earned, jobs she never held, or experience she never had is revealing a dishonesty that should end any consideration, and only verification catches these fabrications. Regulators provide public tools for checking the registration and disciplinary history of investment advisers and brokers, and these should be consulted for anyone being seriously considered.

Below are the main things background verification confirms, and where the information comes from.

What to Verify	Why It Matters	Where to Look
Regulatory history	Reveals past sanctions or disciplinary actions	Public regulatory databases and filings
Litigation record	Uncovers disputes, misconduct, financial trouble	Court records and legal databases
Criminal history	Identifies serious integrity concerns	Background check services
Credentials and employment	Catches lies about degrees and experience	Direct verification with institutions
Prior fund performance	Confirms the track record is real and complete	Cross-checking with independent sources

The purpose of all this human investigation is to assess a quality that determines everything else: integrity. Every other form of due diligence, the track record analysis, the operational review, the examination of terms, ultimately depends on the honesty of the person running the fund. A dishonest manager can fabricate a track record, disguise operational weaknesses, and structure terms to exploit investors, and the numbers alone may not reveal the deception until it's too late, as Madoff proved. Reference checks and background verification are the tools for judging the character that underlies everything, for detecting the integrity problems that would eventually surface as fraud or misconduct. An investor who thoroughly investigates a strategy and operations but never examines the character of the people involved has skipped the assessment that matters most, because in the end, entrusting money to a hedge fund is entrusting it to human beings, and their honesty is the ground on which every other consideration rests.

Discussion Question

Nearly every safeguard in this chapter, the independent administrator, the reputable auditor, the off-list reference, the verified credential, was available to the investors who lost everything with Madoff, and some investors did use these safeguards to correctly avoid him. Yet thousands of intelligent, experienced people, including sophisticated institutions with dedicated due diligence teams, invested anyway, seduced by returns that a careful analyst could see were impossible. If the tools to catch the largest fraud in history already existed and were known, what actually failed, and does that failure suggest the real weakness in due diligence isn't a lack of the right procedures but something about human psychology that no checklist can fix?

Chapter 9: Foundations, Endowments, and Institutional Allocation

An ordinary person saving for retirement holds some mix of stock funds and bond funds, and that's about it. Yale University, at the height of its most celebrated era of investing, held barely a tenth of its money in American stocks and almost nothing in ordinary bonds. The overwhelming majority sat in exactly the alternatives this book has spent eight chapters describing: hedge funds, private equity, venture capital, real estate, and natural resources.

Two investors, the retiree and the university, looking at the same menu of the world's investments, arrived at portfolios so different they barely resemble each other. This chapter is about why the largest and most sophisticated investors on earth build their portfolios the way they do, and what the rest of us can learn from the choices they've made.

Everything covered so far, the individual strategies, the mechanics, the risks, has been about the pieces. This final chapter is about assembling them, about how foundations, university endowments, and pension funds decide how much to put in alternatives, which managers to choose, and how to structure a portfolio meant to last not for years but for centuries. These institutions think in time horizons no individual can match, and that difference in horizon changes everything about how they invest.

We'll look at the theory that underpins modern portfolio construction and where it strains when applied to alternatives, the famous model that David Swensen built at Yale, the choice between accessing managers directly or through intermediaries, the discipline of managing liquidity across a long-lived portfolio, and the growing pressure to weigh values alongside returns.

Modern Portfolio Theory Applied to Alternatives

Every serious conversation about building a portfolio traces back to one idea published in 1952, when a young economist named Harry Markowitz wrote a paper that changed how the world thinks about investing. Before Markowitz, investors evaluated each investment on its own, asking whether this stock or that bond was a good buy. Markowitz shifted the question from the individual investment to the portfolio as a whole, and in doing so he built the mathematical foundation on which nearly all institutional investing still rests. Understanding his framework, and where it holds up and where it cracks when applied to alternatives, is the starting point for thinking about how large investors allocate their money.

Markowitz's central insight was that the risk of a portfolio isn't simply the average of the risks of its holdings, because the holdings partly offset one another. What matters isn't how risky each investment is on its own, but how the investments move in relation to each other. Combine assets that don't move in lockstep, and their independent movements cancel out to some degree, producing a portfolio that's less risky than its individual pieces would suggest. This was a genuine breakthrough. It meant an investor could reduce risk without sacrificing return simply by combining assets thoughtfully, capturing a benefit that comes purely from how holdings interact rather than from picking better individual investments. Markowitz won the Nobel Prize in economics for this work, and the diversification benefit he identified is the reason every large portfolio spreads across many different kinds of assets.

The framework produces a concept called the efficient frontier, which represents the set of portfolios offering the highest possible return for each level of risk. For any amount of risk an investor is willing to accept, there's an optimal portfolio, one that squeezes out the maximum return for that risk, and the collection of all these optimal portfolios forms the frontier. An investor's job, under this framework, is to build a portfolio that sits on the frontier rather than below it, because any portfolio below the frontier is taking more risk than necessary for its return, or earning less return than possible for its risk. The whole exercise of portfolio construction becomes a search for these efficient combinations.

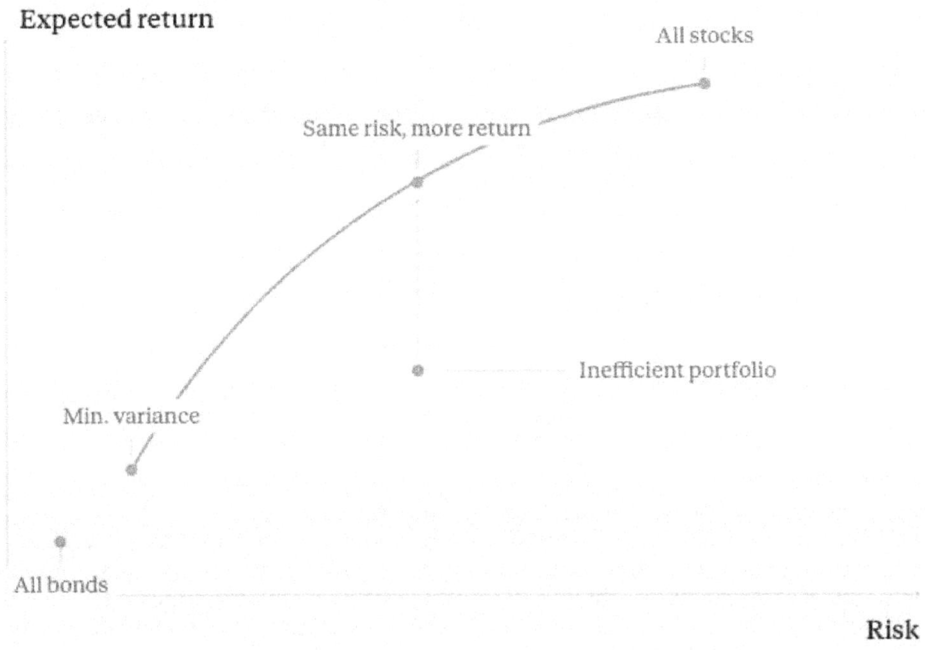

Alternatives enter this framework as a way to push the efficient frontier outward, to reach combinations of risk and return that stocks and bonds alone can't achieve. Because many alternatives have low correlation with traditional assets, as the earlier chapters explored, adding them to a portfolio of stocks and bonds can reduce the portfolio's overall risk or increase its return, moving it to a better position. An investor who holds only stocks and bonds is confined to the frontier those two assets can produce. Adding alternatives that behave differently expands the range of what's possible, potentially delivering the same return with less risk, or more return with the same risk. This is the theoretical justification, in the language of Markowitz, for why sophisticated investors include alternatives at all: they're tools for reaching a more efficient portfolio than traditional assets alone allow.

That's the clean theory, and it's genuinely useful as a way of thinking. But applying Markowitz's framework to alternatives runs into serious problems, and honest institutional investors acknowledge that the theory strains badly when stretched to cover assets it wasn't designed for. Markowitz built his model around publicly traded securities with continuous prices and measurable statistics, and alternatives violate nearly every assumption the model depends on.

Here's where the theory and the reality of alternatives diverge, and why the elegant math becomes unreliable.

MPT Assumption	Reality for Alternatives	Consequence
Prices are observed continuously	Alternatives are priced infrequently, often by estimate	Measured risk is artificially low
Returns follow a normal bell curve	Alternatives have fat tails and extreme outcomes	The model understates the chance of disaster
Correlations are stable	Correlations spike toward one in crises	Diversification fails when it's needed most
Assets can be freely bought and sold	Alternatives are illiquid and locked up	The portfolio can't be rebalanced on demand
Past statistics predict future behavior	Alternative returns are noisy and short-histoired	Estimates are unreliable, especially for risk

Study the first row, because it produces the most pervasive distortion. Markowitz's model measures risk through volatility, the ups and downs of an asset's price. But alternatives are priced infrequently, sometimes only quarterly, and often by appraisal or manager estimate rather than by real market transactions. As discussed earlier, this infrequent pricing makes alternatives appear far less volatile than they truly are, because a price that doesn't move between valuations shows no volatility even when the underlying value is swinging. When this artificially smooth data feeds into Markowitz's model, the model concludes that alternatives are much safer than they actually are, and it recommends allocating more to them than genuine risk would justify. The theory, fed distorted inputs, produces distorted advice.

The second and third rows compound the problem in exactly the way earlier chapters described. The bell curve at the heart of the model badly underestimates extreme events, which strike alternatives hard, and the stable correlations the model assumes break down precisely in the crises when an investor most needs diversification to work. An institution that trusts the model's tidy numbers can believe its portfolio is well-diversified and safe, only to watch every holding fall together when a real crisis arrives, the careful diversification evaporating just as the model's assumptions collapse. The framework is a useful way to organize thinking, but treating its outputs as precise truth, especially for alternatives, is a mistake that has burned many investors who mistook mathematical elegance for reliable prediction.

Sophisticated institutions therefore use Markowitz's framework as a guide rather than a formula, understanding its logic while distrusting its precise numbers. They recognize the genuine benefit of combining assets that behave differently, which is real and worth pursuing, while remaining skeptical of the exact allocations the math produces, because they know the inputs for alternatives are corrupted by infrequent pricing and unstable relationships. The wisdom lies in taking the insight, that diversification across truly different return streams improves a portfolio, without swallowing the false precision, that a model can tell you the optimal percentage to put in each asset down to the decimal point. The best institutional investors hold both ideas at once: the framework is illuminating, and its specific recommendations for alternatives can't be trusted.

The Yale Endowment Model

No single approach has shaped institutional investing over the past several decades more than the model David Swensen built at Yale University, and it deserves the most thorough treatment in this chapter because it represents the fullest expression of how a long-lived institution can use alternatives to transform its results. Swensen took over Yale's endowment in 1985 and ran it until his death in 2021, and over those thirty-six years he produced returns that made Yale the envy of the investing world and inspired institutions everywhere to remake themselves toward what Swensen was doing.

The results were staggering. When Swensen arrived, Yale's endowment held about one billion dollars, invested in the conventional way of the era, mostly in domestic stocks and bonds. By the time of his death, it had grown to over thirty billion dollars, compounding at roughly thirteen to fourteen percent a year over more than three decades, a record almost no other large institution came close to matching. The additional wealth this performance generated for Yale, compared to what a conventional portfolio would have produced, ran into the tens of billions of dollars, money that funded scholarships, professorships, research, and the university's operations. Swensen didn't just beat the market; he redefined what a university endowment could achieve, and he did it by rethinking portfolio construction from the ground up.

The core of Swensen's approach, which came to be called the Yale Model or the endowment model, rested on a handful of connected ideas that together broke sharply from how institutions had always invested. The first idea was a heavy commitment to equity-like investments and a corresponding retreat from bonds and cash. Swensen reasoned that an endowment with an effectively infinite time horizon should own assets that grow over the long run, and that bonds, which merely preserve capital and pay modest interest, were a poor fit for an institution that would exist forever and needed its money to grow. He minimized Yale's holdings of bonds and cash, viewing them as a drag on a portfolio that could afford to prioritize long-term growth over short-term stability.

The second and more radical idea was an enormous allocation to illiquid alternatives, precisely the asset classes this book has examined. Swensen recognized something other institutions had missed: that an endowment's greatest advantage was its ability to tolerate illiquidity. Because Yale would never need to liquidate its entire portfolio and could plan its spending far in advance, it could lock up large portions of its money in investments that individuals and even many institutions couldn't touch. And by accepting that illiquidity, Yale could capture the illiquidity premium discussed in the opening chapter, earning the extra return that comes from giving up the freedom to sell. Swensen poured Yale's money into private equity, venture capital, hedge funds, real estate, and natural resources, embracing the illiquidity that frightened others as a source of advantage rather than a danger to avoid.

The contrast between a traditional institutional portfolio and Yale's model makes the radicalism unmistakable.

Asset Class	Traditional Portfolio	Yale-Style Endowment Model
Domestic stocks	Large, often 50% or more	Small, sometimes under 10%
Bonds and cash	Substantial, 30% to 40%	Minimal, often under 10%
Foreign stocks	Modest	Moderate
Hedge funds (absolute return)	Little or none	Large, often 20% or more
Private equity and venture capital	Little or none	Large, a cornerstone
Real estate and natural resources	Little or none	Substantial

Look at how completely the two portfolios differ. The traditional portfolio is dominated by domestic stocks and bonds, the familiar holdings of a conventional investor. The Yale model relegates domestic stocks and bonds to minor roles and fills the portfolio with alternatives, inverting the entire structure. An institution following the Yale model holds most of its wealth in exactly the illiquid, lightly regulated, hard-to-access strategies that most investors avoid, betting that these alternatives will deliver superior long-term returns and that the institution's long horizon lets it safely bear their illiquidity.

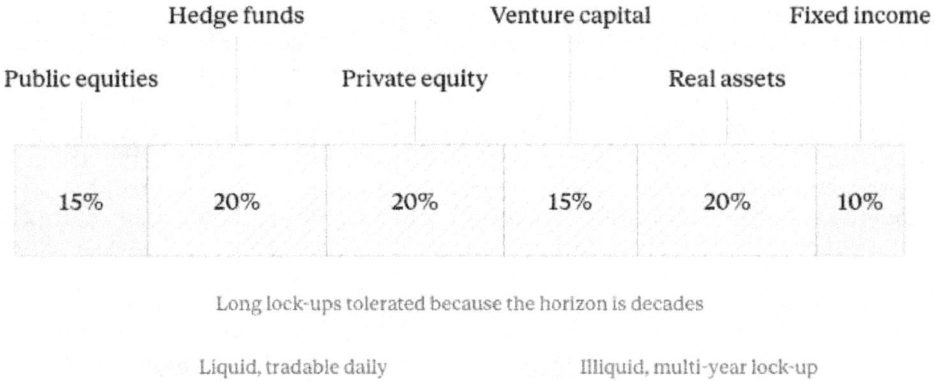

The third pillar of Swensen's approach was a strong belief in active management within alternatives, coupled with a recognition that active management is pointless in efficient public markets. This distinction was subtle and important. Swensen argued that in highly efficient markets, like the market for large American stocks, it's extremely hard for any manager to beat the index, so an investor there should just buy cheap index funds rather than pay for active management that won't add value. But in the inefficient, opaque markets of alternatives, where information is scarce and pricing is imperfect, a skilled manager can find real advantages, so paying for top-tier active management in those areas is worthwhile. Yale therefore indexed its public market holdings cheaply while spending heavily to access the very best managers in private equity, venture capital, and other alternatives, concentrating its effort and fees where skill could actually make a difference.

This led to the fourth pillar: Yale's relentless focus on identifying and accessing elite managers. Swensen understood that in alternatives, the gap between the best managers and the average ones is enormous, far larger than in public markets. In venture capital especially, the top handful of firms capture most of the industry's returns, while the rest deliver mediocre or poor results. Getting into the best funds, therefore, mattered more than almost anything else, and Yale built deep, long-standing relationships with premier managers, becoming a favored investor that top funds wanted in their pool. The university's reputation, its patient capital, and its early recognition of talented managers gave it access to funds that were closed to most investors, and this access to the best became one of its central advantages. The Yale model isn't just about allocating to alternatives; it's about reaching the elite tier of alternative managers that most investors can never touch.

Swensen laid out his philosophy in a book called Pioneering Portfolio Management, published in 2000, which became something close to scripture for institutional investors. The book explained his reasoning in detail, and it inspired a wave of imitation as endowments, foundations, and other institutions rushed to adopt the Yale model, shifting their portfolios toward alternatives in hopes of replicating Yale's success. By the 2000s, the endowment model had become the dominant approach among large university endowments, and Swensen's influence spread far beyond Yale to reshape how a whole category of institutions invested.

But the rush to imitate Yale revealed a hard truth that Swensen himself had warned about: the model is much harder to execute than it looks, and copying its allocations without its execution can fail badly. The reason is that Yale's success depended heavily on its access to elite managers, and most institutions couldn't replicate that access. When lesser institutions adopted the Yale allocations, pouring money into alternatives, they often ended up in mediocre funds rather than the best funds Yale could reach, because the best funds were closed to them or they lacked the skill to identify tomorrow's winners. The result was that many imitators captured the illiquidity and the high fees of alternatives without capturing the superior returns, because they invested with average managers rather than exceptional ones. Swensen was explicit about this danger, cautioning that his approach worked only for institutions that could access top-tier managers, and that ordinary investors trying to copy it would likely be better off with a simple, low-cost portfolio of index funds. The model wasn't a formula anyone could apply; it was an approach that demanded resources, relationships, and judgment that few possessed.

The 2008 financial crisis delivered the sternest test of the endowment model, and it exposed a vulnerability at the model's heart. As markets collapsed, endowments heavy with illiquid alternatives discovered that their illiquidity, the very feature Swensen had turned into an advantage, could become a serious danger when cash was suddenly needed. Yale's endowment fell roughly twenty-five percent in the crisis, and Harvard's fell about twenty-seven percent, enormous losses for institutions that had believed their diversified portfolios would hold up better.

Worse than the paper losses was the liquidity crisis that followed. These institutions had ongoing spending commitments, funding a large share of their universities' budgets, and they'd also made commitments to invest more capital in private equity and other funds, commitments that came due regardless of market conditions. With much of their money locked in illiquid investments that couldn't be sold, and with their liquid holdings shrunken by the crash, some of the wealthiest institutions in the world found themselves scrambling for cash.

The measures they took revealed how severe the squeeze had become. Harvard was forced to issue bonds, borrowing money to meet its obligations because it couldn't access its own frozen wealth. It also tried to sell portions of its private equity holdings on the secondary market, where investors trade existing stakes in private funds, but in the depths of the crisis buyers would only pay steep discounts, so selling meant accepting large losses. The endowment model's reliance on illiquidity, which had generated years of superior returns, suddenly looked like a dangerous flaw when the institutions couldn't turn their assets into cash at the moment they needed it most.

The crisis taught a lesson that reshaped how institutions think about the model: the illiquidity premium is real, but so is illiquidity risk, and an institution that locks up too much of its money can find itself unable to meet its obligations in a crisis, forced to borrow or to sell at fire-sale prices. The episode led many institutions to manage their liquidity far more carefully afterward, a discipline the next section examines directly.

Even with these lessons, the endowment model remains influential, and Yale's long-term record stands as evidence that the approach can work brilliantly in the right hands. The model's core insights, that a long horizon permits bearing illiquidity, that alternatives can improve a diversified portfolio, that elite active management is worth paying for in inefficient markets, remain sound. What the crisis added was a crucial qualification: these advantages must be balanced against the liquidity needs and obligations that even a long-lived institution can't ignore. The best practitioners of the endowment model today pursue Swensen's strategy while maintaining enough liquidity to survive a crisis without being forced to sell, having learned that the model's greatest strength contains its greatest risk.

Fund-of-Funds vs. Direct Manager Access

Once an institution decides to invest in hedge funds and other alternatives, it faces a practical choice about how to do it: invest directly with individual managers, choosing each one itself, or invest through a fund-of-funds, an intermediary that pools investors' money and spreads it across many underlying managers. This choice shapes the cost, the complexity, and the results of the whole alternatives program, and the right answer depends heavily on the resources and sophistication of the investor.

A fund-of-funds is exactly what its name suggests: a fund that invests in other funds. Rather than picking individual hedge funds, an investor puts money into a fund-of-funds, and the managers of that vehicle select a portfolio of underlying hedge funds on the investor's behalf. The fund-of-funds handles the work of finding managers, conducting due diligence, allocating across strategies, and monitoring the investments, delivering the investor a diversified portfolio of hedge funds through a single relationship. For an investor without the expertise or resources to select and monitor individual hedge funds, this arrangement offers a way to access alternatives without doing the demanding work directly.

The appeal of fund-of-funds is straightforward, and it centers on several genuine benefits.

The first is diversification: a fund-of-funds spreads money across many managers and strategies, so the failure or underperformance of any single manager doesn't devastate the investor, providing a layer of protection that investing with just a few managers directly can't match.

The second is professional selection and due diligence: the fund-of-funds employs specialists who evaluate managers, perform the operational and background investigation that earlier chapters described, and make selection decisions that an unsophisticated investor couldn't make well on their own.

The third is access: fund-of-funds sometimes hold positions in elite funds that are closed to new investors, letting their clients reach managers they couldn't access directly.

The fourth is a lower barrier to entry, since a fund-of-funds may accept smaller investments than the large minimums that top individual hedge funds demand.

Against these benefits stands one enormous drawback that has driven many sophisticated investors away from fund-of-funds: an additional layer of fees stacked on top of the already high fees of the underlying hedge funds. This is the problem of fees on fees, and the arithmetic is brutal.

Fee Layer	Typical Charge	Applied To
Underlying hedge funds	2% management, 20% performance	The investor's money at each fund
Fund-of-funds	1% management, 10% performance	The investor's money again, on top
Combined burden	Roughly 3% and 30% in a good year	Devastating to net returns over time

Read what that stacking does. The underlying hedge funds already charge their 2 percent and 20 percent. The fund-of-funds then adds its own fee, often around 1 percent and 10 percent, on top of the underlying fees. The investor ends up paying both layers, so in a good year the total fee burden might approach 3 percent of assets plus 30 percent of profits. Fees of that magnitude are extraordinarily difficult to overcome. For the investor to earn a decent net return, the underlying managers must generate enough to cover two full layers of fees and still leave something worthwhile, a high bar that many fund-of-funds fail to clear. Over years, this double layer of fees compounds into a massive drag, and it's the central reason critics argue fund-of-funds often deliver disappointing net returns despite their other benefits.

The alternative is direct manager access, where the investor selects and invests with individual hedge funds itself, paying only the single layer of fees the underlying funds charge and avoiding the fund-of-funds markup. This is the path Yale and other sophisticated institutions took, building the internal expertise to choose managers directly and cutting out the intermediary. The advantages are lower fees, greater control over which managers the portfolio holds, and direct relationships with the managers themselves. But direct access demands enormous resources: a skilled internal investment team capable of finding, evaluating, and monitoring managers, the ability to meet the large minimum investments top funds require, and the sophistication to perform the due diligence that separates good managers from frauds and failures. Only large, well-resourced institutions can realistically pursue direct access across a full alternatives portfolio, because the work of doing it well is beyond the reach of smaller or less sophisticated investors.

The choice between these two paths comes down to a trade-off between cost and capability. An investor with the resources and expertise to select managers well should generally go direct, avoiding the extra fees and keeping control, as Yale did to great effect. An investor lacking that capability may be better served by a fund-of-funds despite its fees, because a fund-of-funds that selects good managers is preferable to picking bad managers directly and suffering the losses that poor selection brings. The fund-of-funds fees buy expertise and diversification that an unsophisticated investor genuinely needs, and for such an investor, paying for competent selection may be worth more than the fees it costs. The industry has seen many investors move from fund-of-funds toward direct investing as they built internal capabilities and grew frustrated with the double fees, but fund-of-funds retain a role for those who can't or won't do the work themselves. The right answer isn't universal; it depends on whether the investor can do better on their own than the intermediary can do for them, after accounting for the intermediary's fees.

Liquidity Budgeting for Long-Term Investors

The 2008 liquidity crisis that battered even Yale and Harvard taught institutional investors a lesson they've since built into the core of how they manage their portfolios: illiquidity must be managed deliberately, budgeted like any other resource, so that the institution can always meet its obligations without being forced to sell at the worst possible time. Liquidity budgeting is the discipline of ensuring an investor holds enough accessible cash and sellable assets to cover its needs, even while committing large portions of its portfolio to illiquid alternatives. It's the practical safeguard that lets an institution pursue the endowment model's illiquid strategy without falling into the trap that ensnared so many institutions in the crisis.

The problem liquidity budgeting solves is a mismatch between an institution's obligations and its assets. Institutions have ongoing needs for cash: endowments fund a large share of their universities' operating budgets, foundations must pay out grants, pension funds must send checks to retirees, and all of them have committed to invest additional capital in private funds over time, commitments called capital calls that come due on the fund managers' schedule, not the institution's.

Meanwhile, much of the institution's wealth may be locked in illiquid alternatives that can't be quickly converted to cash. If the institution hasn't planned carefully, it can find itself owing money, through spending needs and capital calls, while unable to access enough of its own wealth to pay, exactly the bind Harvard faced in 2008. Liquidity budgeting exists to prevent that bind by ensuring the institution always has enough accessible resources to meet its obligations.

The practice works by organizing the portfolio into tiers based on how quickly each holding can be turned into cash, and then ensuring the institution holds enough in the more liquid tiers to cover its foreseeable needs. This tiering makes the portfolio's true liquidity visible and lets the institution plan around it.

Liquidity Tier	Examples	Role in the Budget
Immediate	Cash, money market funds	Covers near-term spending and emergencies
Highly liquid	Public stocks, government bonds	Can be sold within days if needed

Semi-liquid	Hedge funds with periodic redemptions	Accessible on the fund's redemption schedule
Illiquid	Private equity, venture capital, real estate	Locked up for years, can't be counted on for cash

The essential principle is matching the portfolio's liquidity to the institution's obligations, ensuring that the cash needs over any given period can be met from the liquid tiers without touching the illiquid holdings. An institution must know how much cash it will need for spending and capital calls over the coming years, and it must hold enough in the immediate and highly liquid tiers to cover those needs with a margin of safety. The illiquid tier, however attractive its returns, can't be relied upon to produce cash on demand, so it must be sized so that the institution never depends on selling it to meet obligations. Getting this balance right lets an institution hold a large allocation to illiquid alternatives while remaining confident it can always pay its bills, capturing the illiquidity premium without courting the illiquidity crisis.

A particular danger that liquidity budgeting must account for is the way liquidity needs and market crises tend to strike at the same time, compounding each other. In a crisis, several bad things happen at once. The institution's spending needs may rise or stay constant while its liquid assets shrink in value, capital calls from private funds may accelerate as those funds move to buy distressed assets, and the illiquid holdings become even harder to sell as markets freeze. All of these pressures converge precisely when the institution can least afford them, which is what turned 2008 from a paper-loss event into a genuine liquidity crisis for institutions that hadn't budgeted conservatively. Prudent liquidity budgeting therefore plans not for normal conditions but for stressed ones, holding enough liquidity to survive a crisis in which everything goes wrong simultaneously, because that's exactly the scenario in which running out of cash proves catastrophic. The institutions that learned this lesson from 2008 now stress-test their liquidity, asking whether they could meet all their obligations even in a severe crisis without being forced to sell illiquid assets at a loss, and they hold their allocations accordingly.

ESG Integration in Alternative Investment Mandates

The newest force reshaping how institutions invest has nothing to do with returns in the traditional sense. It concerns whether investors should weigh the environmental, social, and governance consequences of their investments alongside financial results, and it has grown from a fringe concern into a central debate that every large institution now confronts. ESG, standing for environmental, social, and governance, refers to a set of non-financial factors that investors increasingly consider, and its application to alternatives raises genuine questions about the purpose of investing that reasonable people answer very differently.

The three components of ESG cover distinct concerns. The environmental dimension addresses a company's impact on the natural world: its carbon emissions, its pollution, its use of resources, its exposure to climate risk. The social dimension covers a company's relationships with people: its treatment of workers, its labor practices, its effect on the communities where it operates, its handling of customer welfare and product safety. The governance dimension concerns how a company is run: the independence and accountability of its board, the alignment of executive pay with performance, the transparency of its practices, and its vulnerability to corruption or self-dealing. Together these factors describe dimensions of a company's behavior and risk that traditional financial analysis, focused purely on profits and cash flows, might overlook.

Investors approach ESG in several distinct ways, and distinguishing among them clarifies a debate that often blurs different practices together.

Approach	What It Does	Underlying Goal
Negative screening	Excludes certain industries or companies entirely	Avoid profiting from objectionable businesses
ESG integration	Weighs ESG factors alongside financial ones in analysis	Improve returns by capturing overlooked risks
Thematic investing	Targets investments in specific ESG themes	Direct capital toward chosen goals like clean energy
Impact investing	Seeks measurable social or environmental impact	Achieve real-world change alongside financial return

These approaches rest on different logic, and the difference matters for the debate. Negative screening simply refuses to invest in certain businesses, tobacco, weapons, fossil fuels, on moral grounds, accepting whatever financial cost that refusal carries as the price of not profiting from objectionable activity. ESG integration is different and financially motivated: it argues that ESG factors represent real risks that traditional analysis misses, and that weighing them improves returns by identifying dangers, a company facing environmental liabilities, labor unrest, or governance scandals, that could hurt its financial performance. Under this view, ESG isn't about values at all but about better risk assessment, capturing information that helps predict which companies will stumble. Thematic and impact investing go further, actively directing capital toward environmental or social goals, sometimes accepting lower returns in exchange for real-world effect. The debate over ESG often conflates these distinct approaches, treating a financially motivated risk-assessment practice as if it were the same as sacrificing returns for values, when they rest on entirely different reasoning.

The tension at the heart of the ESG debate is a genuine conflict between two views of what an institutional investor is supposed to do, and it's sharpened for institutions like pensions and endowments that manage money on behalf of others. On one side stands the argument from fiduciary duty: that an institution managing money for beneficiaries, retirees depending on a pension, students depending on an endowment, has an obligation to maximize financial returns for those beneficiaries, and that sacrificing returns to pursue social or environmental goals betrays that duty.

Under this view, an endowment exists to fund the university, not to advance the trustees' political preferences, and using the beneficiaries' money to pursue values rather than returns is a breach of the institution's core responsibility. On the other side stands the argument that investors can't ignore their impact on the world, that beneficiaries may genuinely want their money invested in line with their values, and that ignoring ESG risks is itself financially irresponsible because those risks are real. This clash, between the duty to maximize returns and the desire to invest responsibly, has no easy resolution, and institutions have landed on different sides of it.

David Swensen himself weighed in on this question, and his position was characteristically nuanced. He argued that ethical considerations did have a place in endowment investing, that a university couldn't entirely divorce its investments from its values, but he also insisted that ethical investing be pursued carefully and not used as an excuse for poor financial decisions.

Swensen pressed Yale's managers on issues like climate change, asking them to consider the risks that carbon-intensive investments carried, framing it partly as a matter of financial prudence and partly as a matter of the university's responsibilities. His approach reflected the difficulty of the question: he neither dismissed values as irrelevant to investing nor let them override the financial discipline that made Yale successful, trying instead to hold both concerns in balance.

Norway's sovereign wealth fund offers one of the clearest examples of ESG applied at institutional scale, and it shows how a large investor can build ethical considerations into its process systematically. The fund, which manages the wealth Norway accumulated from its oil reserves and ranks among the largest investors in the world, operates under a set of ethical guidelines overseen by a dedicated Council on Ethics. The council recommends excluding companies that violate the fund's ethical standards, and the fund has excluded businesses involved in certain weapons, severe environmental damage, serious human rights violations, and, more recently, significant coal operations. This structured, transparent approach to ethical exclusion, applied consistently across an enormous portfolio, demonstrates that a major institution can integrate values into its investing in a disciplined way, though even Norway's approach involves constant debate about which exclusions are justified and what they cost in returns.

The application of ESG to alternatives raises particular challenges that make it harder than in public markets. Public companies increasingly disclose ESG data, letting investors assess their environmental, social, and governance practices, but the private companies and funds that populate alternatives disclose far less, making ESG assessment difficult where information is scarce. A private equity fund's portfolio companies may not report their carbon emissions or labor practices, and a hedge fund may not reveal enough about its holdings for an investor to judge their ESG characteristics. This opacity, one of the defining features of alternatives throughout this book, complicates ESG efforts by depriving investors of the data they'd need to evaluate their alternative holdings against ESG standards. Institutions committed to ESG have pushed their alternative managers to disclose more and to consider ESG factors in their own investing, but the private nature of alternatives makes this an ongoing struggle rather than a solved problem.

ESG has also generated a strong backlash, and honesty requires presenting this opposition alongside the case for ESG, because the debate has become genuinely contested along political lines. Critics argue that ESG investing sacrifices returns for political goals, breaching the fiduciary duty to beneficiaries, and that it lets asset managers impose their own values on money that isn't theirs. Some contend that ESG ratings are inconsistent and unreliable, measuring different things at different providers and offering no coherent standard.

In the United States, this opposition has taken concrete form, with several states moving to pull money from asset managers over their ESG practices, arguing that those managers were prioritizing political agendas over financial returns for state pensioners. Some states passed laws restricting the use of ESG factors in managing public money, while others pushed in the opposite direction, requiring consideration of climate and other risks. The result is a genuinely divided environment in which ESG is embraced in some quarters and actively resisted in others, and where an institution's stance on ESG has itself become a politically charged decision. Whether ESG represents prudent risk management, a values-driven improvement to investing, or an inappropriate intrusion of politics into finance remains fiercely disputed, and the answer an institution gives depends on its beneficiaries, its jurisdiction, and its own judgment about the purpose of the money it manages.

What ties ESG back to everything else in this chapter is that it's ultimately another question of portfolio construction, another factor institutions must weigh as they decide how to allocate money meant to serve their beneficiaries and endure across time. The institutional investor assembling a portfolio of alternatives must now consider not only expected returns, risk, correlation, liquidity, and manager quality, but also whether and how to account for the environmental, social, and governance consequences of where the money goes. For the foundations, endowments, and pension funds that deploy capital into the strategies this book has examined, the work of allocation has grown more complex, encompassing both the timeless questions of risk and return and the newer, contested questions of values and impact, all in service of institutions built to last far longer than any individual investor's horizon.

Discussion Question

The Yale model worked spectacularly for Yale, yet Swensen himself warned that most institutions copying it would fail, because they lacked the access to top managers that made his results possible, and many imitators did capture the fees and illiquidity of alternatives without the superior returns. This raises an uncomfortable possibility: that the strategy's success depended less on the alternatives themselves than on advantages, reputation, relationships, early recognition of talent, that can't be copied and may not even be repeatable by Yale in a more crowded and competitive market.

If the returns came from privileged access rather than from the asset classes, what does that mean for the thousands of institutions and individuals who have restructured their portfolios around the endowment model, and how would an institution honestly know whether it possesses the rare advantages the model requires or is merely paying high fees for the illusion of them?

Conclusion

We began this book with a simple puzzle: what makes an investment "alternative," and why do the wealthiest, most sophisticated investors on earth pour so much money into strategies most people can't access and few understand? The answer should feel less mysterious now. Alternatives aren't a single exotic product or a secret path to easy riches. They're a broad collection of strategies that share a few traits, lighter regulation, harder access, less liquidity, and returns that often behave differently from stocks and bonds. That last trait, the different behavior, turns out to be the point.

If there's one idea worth carrying away from these nine chapters, it's that the value of a hedge fund often has little to do with beating the market. A steady 6 percent that shows up whether stocks soar or crash can be worth more inside a portfolio than a flashy 15 percent that rises and falls with everything else you own. Independence is the product. A return that zigs when the rest of your money zags is what lets a large institution survive the crash that wipes out the investor who owned only one kind of risk.

You've also seen the other side, and this book tried to stay honest about it. Fees are steep, and they've often outrun the results that once justified them. Most managers don't deliver the pure absolute return they promise. Leverage that magnifies gains magnifies ruin just as fast, as Long-Term Capital Management learned with a roster of Nobel laureates. Correlations that protect you in calm markets vanish in the panics when you need them most. Backtests that look perfect can be monuments to noise. And the smooth, impossible track record that seduced thousands of Madoff's investors was the very thing that should have warned them off.

The strategies themselves ran across a wide range. Long/short managers buy the good and short the bad. Macro traders bet on whole economies. Event-driven funds profit from mergers and bankruptcies. Quants let mathematics find patterns no human could track. Each has an edge, and each has a way it breaks, usually the same way: a rare, severe loss hiding behind a long stretch of steady gains.

What ties everything together is a discipline that has nothing to do with cleverness and everything to do with survival. The managers who last aren't the ones who are right most often. They're the ones who structure their risk so that being wrong, which is guaranteed, can't kill them. The investors who last aren't the ones who chase last year's best returns. They're the ones who ask where the returns came from, who holds the money, and what happens when the crisis arrives.

You don't need to run a hedge fund to use any of this. The habits that protect a billion-dollar endowment, spreading risk across truly different bets, questioning smooth results, matching your commitments to what you can afford to lock away, protect anyone. The greatest edge in finance has never been finding certainty, but learning how to prosper without needing it.

Example Answers to End-of-Chapter Questions

Chapter 1: Is wealth a defensible proxy for the sophistication these markets require, and how would you redesign access?

Wealth is a poor proxy for sophistication, and everyone knows it. A lottery winner qualifies while a finance PhD earning a modest salary does not. The rules confuse the ability to survive a loss with the ability to understand one, and those are different things. If I were redesigning the system, I'd separate the two questions. Anyone could demonstrate sophistication through a rigorous exam covering risk, illiquidity, and fees, unlocking access regardless of net worth, which is the direction the 2020 addition of licensed professionals started to move. But I'd keep a separate loss-absorption test too, because understanding a risk doesn't mean you can afford it. Here's what my approach would get wrong that the current one gets right: a crude wealth line is cheap to administer, hard to game, and genuinely does ensure that people who lose everything in a fund won't be left destitute. An exam-based system invites coaching, credential mills, and people who pass the test but still can't afford the loss. The current rule is unfair and blunt, but its bluntness is also its protection.

Chapter 2: How should you weight the management fee against the performance fee to align incentives, and what breaks at the extremes?

Push toward the performance fee and away from the management fee, because only the performance fee pays the manager when you win. But you can't go all the way. A fund with a tiny management fee and a huge performance share creates a dangerous incentive: the manager collects a fifth of the upside but eats none of the downside, so she's tempted to swing wildly, since a lucky year makes her rich and a terrible year costs her only the fees she wasn't collecting anyway. Strip the management fee too low and you also starve the operation, forcing the manager to gather assets just to keep the lights on. Strip the performance fee too low and she has no reason to excel. The real fix isn't the ratio at all. It's pairing a modest management fee with a high-water mark and a large personal investment from the manager, so she genuinely shares your losses.

Chapter 3: When is a decorrelated but lower-returning strategy earning its place, versus using "low correlation" as an excuse for mediocrity?

This is the hardest judgment in portfolio construction, because the honest answer requires distinguishing two things that look identical in a good year. A market-neutral fund returning 6 percent and a mediocre fund hiding behind the same number both trail the index, and both claim their independence justifies the gap. The way to tell them apart is to examine the correlation itself, not the return. Genuine decorrelation is stable and shows up when it matters. A fund earning its place will hold its ground, or better, during the market's worst stretches, which is precisely when its independence pays off. If it fell right alongside stocks in 2008 and 2020, its "low correlation" was a calm-weather illusion, and you're paying hedge fund fees for hidden beta. So the test has two parts. First, does the return stream stay uncorrelated under stress, or only when nothing is happening? Second, and this is where investors fail, are you measuring the fund against the right benchmark? Comparing an absolute return fund to the S&P 500 in a bull market is a category error that will make even a good fund look bad and tempt you to abandon it at the worst moment. The fee question is separate and harsh: even a genuinely decorrelated 6 percent may not survive a 2-and-20 structure, because after fees there's little diversification benefit left to justify the cost. Low correlation earns its place only when it's real, durable in a crisis, and cheap enough that the benefit reaches you rather than the manager.

Chapter 4: Systematic or discretionary for the next twenty years, and what does your choice reveal?

I'd split the money, but if forced to choose one, I'd lean discretionary, and the choice reveals that I fear machine rigidity more than human weakness. Twenty years guarantees events no model has seen, and a system trained on the past can fail catastrophically when the present stops resembling it. A thoughtful human can at least recognize that the world has changed. But I hold this loosely, because the honest reason most people pick discretionary is overconfidence in judgment, theirs or their manager's, and that same confidence is what blows people up. My real answer is that the question is a false binary, and the funds worth trusting use both.

Chapter 5: How can you distinguish a skilled event-driven manager from one who's just been lucky before the inevitable loss, and can it even be known in advance?

You mostly can't know for certain in advance, and pretending otherwise is how investors get hurt. The strategy's structure, many small wins and rare large losses, means a manager who's simply been collecting spreads while the bad event hasn't arrived looks identical to a genuinely skilled one right up until the break. Both show smooth, steady gains. That said, there are ways to shift the odds. Examine the losses the manager has already taken, because every experienced event-driven manager has broken deals in her history, and how she sized those positions tells you whether she respects the asymmetry or ignores it. A manager who has never had a meaningful loss is more worrying than one who has, because the loss-free record suggests either a short track record or hidden risk-taking that hasn't detonated yet. Ask how she sizes positions relative to the downside if the event fails, not the upside if it succeeds. Skill shows up in position sizing and process, in whether a single broken deal could cripple her, far more than in the string of wins. But the deepest answer is uncomfortable: the difference between skill and luck in this strategy often can't be proven until the severe loss arrives and reveals whether she survived it by design or avoided it by chance.

Chapter 6: Given that the future is the only real test of a quant strategy, what justifies funding one at all, and how much of quants' confidence is just sophisticated overfitting?

What justifies funding a quant strategy isn't the backtest, which proves almost nothing, but the reason the pattern should exist. A strategy backed by a genuine economic or behavioral cause, investors underreacting to news, a structural feature of how a market clears, has a claim on the future that a pattern discovered by pure data-mining does not. The out-of-sample test helps, and paper trading helps, but neither is proof. The honest position is that funding a quant strategy is always a bet that a documented past pattern rests on something durable rather than on coincidence, and you can never fully verify which until real money has been at risk. As for how much of quants' confidence is disguised overfitting: probably more than they'd admit. The discipline of holding out data and demanding a rationale exists precisely because the temptation to fool yourself is overwhelming, and the fact that serious quants build elaborate defenses against self-deception is itself evidence of how easily the field deceives itself.

Chapter 7: Where's the line between the discipline that keeps a fund alive and the caution that makes it pointless, and can you know which side you're on before the crisis?

There's no fixed line, and that's the genuinely hard part. Too much leverage and too little are both fatal, one fast and one slow. LTCM died from too much, unable to survive being temporarily wrong. A fund that uses no leverage, caps every position tightly, and takes minimal risk dies differently, from returns so unremarkable that investors leave for cheaper index funds. Both are failures. The line between them isn't a number you can calculate in advance, because it depends on a crisis whose severity you can't know until it arrives. What you can do is reason about survival directly rather than about returns. The right question isn't "how much can I make?" but "what's the worst plausible move against me, and would it end the fund?" A manager who has honestly answered that question, who has stress-tested her portfolio against catastrophes worse than any in the historical data, and who still has room to endure them, is on the right side of the line even if she can't prove it. The trap is that this reasoning always feels too cautious during good times, when leverage is cheap and the last crisis is a fading memory, and it always feels obviously correct afterward. The managers who survive tend to be the ones who accept looking overly cautious for years as the price of being present when the test comes.

But here's the uncomfortable truth the question points at: you can construct your risk so carefully that you're confident you'd survive, and still discover that the actual crisis was worse than anything you modeled. The line can only be located precisely in hindsight, which is exactly why the discipline has to be maintained before you can see it.

Chapter 8: If the tools to catch Madoff already existed and were known, what actually failed, and is the real weakness in due diligence something no checklist can fix?

What failed wasn't the availability of the tools but the willingness to use them against a manager whose returns everyone wanted to believe. The red flags, self-custody, a three-person auditor, impossibly smooth returns, were visible to anyone who looked, and the investors who did the operational work avoided him. The ones who lost everything skipped it, dazzled by the consistency and by the social proof of other smart people investing. So yes, the deepest weakness is psychological, not procedural. A checklist only works if you run it, and the pull to skip it grows stronger exactly as an opportunity looks more attractive and more people vouch for it. The lesson isn't that we need better procedures. It's that the moment you most want to believe in a manager is the moment you most need to force yourself through the boring verification you'd rather skip.

Chapter 9: If Yale's returns came from privileged access rather than the asset classes themselves, what does that mean for everyone who copied the model, and how would an institution know which it has?

If the returns came from access rather than from alternatives as a category, then most institutions and individuals who restructured around the endowment model made a mistake, and Swensen said as much himself. They adopted Yale's allocations, the heavy tilt into private equity, venture capital, and hedge funds, without Yale's ability to reach the elite managers who actually generated the outperformance. What they captured instead was the illiquidity and the high fees, paired with average managers whose returns didn't justify either. That's the worst outcome: locking up your money and paying premium prices for mediocre results dressed up as sophistication. Knowing which situation you're in is genuinely hard, because access feels like skill from the inside, and every institution believes it can identify tomorrow's top funds.

The honest test is brutal and mostly retrospective – are you consistently getting into funds that are closed to others, and do your alternative managers actually beat cheap public alternatives after all fees, measured over a long enough period to rule out luck? If you can't demonstrate real access to funds others can't reach, and your alternatives aren't clearly outperforming a simple index portfolio after fees, you probably don't have the advantages the model requires. Most institutions can't demonstrate this, which suggests most are paying for the illusion. The uncomfortable implication is that for the majority of investors, the right response to Yale's success was never to copy it, but to recognize that its central ingredient couldn't be copied at all, and to build a cheaper, simpler portfolio instead.

Historical Timeline of Hedge Funds

1949. The story starts with a sociologist and journalist named Alfred Winslow Jones, who launched what most people regard as the first hedge fund. Working for Fortune magazine, Jones grew convinced that a smarter way to invest existed, and he tested it with a structure nobody had combined before. He bought stocks he expected to rise, shorted stocks he expected to fall, and borrowed money to amplify both bets. The shorting "hedged" his exposure to the overall market, so his returns depended more on his stock picking than on the market's direction, and the borrowing magnified the results. He also took a 20 percent share of profits, planting the seed of a fee convention that would outlive him by generations. For years almost nobody noticed.

1966. Then Carol Loomis wrote an article in Fortune titled "The Jones Nobody Keeps Up With," and everything changed. She revealed that Jones's fund had trounced the best mutual funds of the era over both five and ten years, even after his fees. Money and imitators flooded in.

1968. By the time the Securities and Exchange Commission surveyed the field, it counted roughly 140 hedge funds, a small industry that had sprung up almost overnight in the wake of Jones's exposure. Managers who understood the structure, and many who didn't, rushed to launch funds and capture the returns Jones had demonstrated.

1969 to 1974. The first boom met the first reckoning. A brutal bear market ran through these years, and many of the new funds, it turned out, had understood only half of Jones's model. They loved the borrowing that magnified gains but neglected the disciplined shorting that was supposed to protect them, so when stocks fell, their leverage magnified losses instead. A large share of the funds launched in the excitement of the late 1960s simply vanished, wiped out by the very leverage that had made them look brilliant on the way up. The episode delivered a lesson the industry would relearn many times: leverage cuts both ways, and a strategy that ignores its downside is a disaster waiting for a bad market.

1975. Ray Dalio founded Bridgewater Associates out of his New York apartment, beginning what would become one of the largest hedge fund firms in the world, built on his systematic approach to understanding economies as machines driven by debt cycles.

1980. A remarkable year for the industry's future. Julian Robertson founded Tiger Management, and Paul Tudor Jones founded Tudor Investment Corporation, two firms that would define the aggressive, talent-driven hedge fund culture of the coming decades. Robertson became famous for his stock-picking prowess and for training a generation of managers who came to be called the Tiger Cubs. Jones built his reputation on macro trading and an almost obsessive focus on risk.

1982. James Simons, a decorated mathematician who had done code-breaking work and led a university math department, founded Renaissance Technologies, a firm that would take the quantitative approach further than anyone imagined possible.

1986. The decade's darker side surfaced when Ivan Boesky, one of the most celebrated risk arbitrage traders on Wall Street, was exposed for illegal insider trading. Boesky had made enormous profits trading merger situations, and it emerged that much of his edge came from buying targets based on advance, illegal knowledge of deals before they were announced. His guilty plea and cooperation with prosecutors cracked open a wider insider trading scandal, and his downfall cast a shadow over merger arbitrage, though the legitimate version of the strategy, based on public analysis, endured.

1987. On October 19, a day remembered as Black Monday, stock markets around the world crashed with terrifying speed, the largest single-day percentage drop in the history of the American market. Amid the wreckage, Paul Tudor Jones became a legend by anticipating the crash and positioning to profit from it, reportedly earning huge returns while most investors were devastated. The crash showed what a skilled macro trader could do with a correct read on a coming disaster.

1988. Renaissance Technologies launched its Medallion fund, which would go on to post returns so consistent and so high, roughly 66 percent a year before fees over the following decades, that they redefined what was thought achievable and made Simons one of the wealthiest people in finance.

1990. Ken Griffin founded Citadel, having started out trading convertible bonds from his Harvard dorm room. The firm grew from that narrow technical edge into one of the largest and most successful hedge fund operations in existence.

1992. George Soros executed the most famous trade in hedge fund history. Convinced that Britain couldn't sustain its commitment to a fixed exchange rate, Soros, with Stanley Druckenmiller managing the position, bet enormously against the British pound. On September 16, a day the British press called Black Wednesday, Britain gave up defending the currency and let it collapse. Soros's Quantum Fund reportedly earned around a billion dollars in days, and he became known as the man who broke the Bank of England, a vivid demonstration of macro trading at its most audacious.

1994. John Meriwether, a legendary bond trader, founded Long-Term Capital Management, assembling what looked like the smartest team ever gathered in finance, including the economists Myron Scholes and Robert Merton. The firm's strategy exploited tiny pricing discrepancies between related bonds, magnified by enormous leverage.

1997. Scholes and Merton won the Nobel Prize in economics for their work on pricing options, cementing LTCM's aura of invincibility just as an Asian financial crisis began rattling markets and hinting at the turmoil to come.

1998. The invincible fund fell. When Russia defaulted on its debt, an event LTCM's models treated as nearly impossible, panic swept through exactly the positions the fund held, and its extreme leverage turned modest adverse moves into catastrophic losses. Within weeks LTCM had lost most of its capital, and its positions were so large that the Federal Reserve organized a rescue by major banks to unwind the fund without dragging down the whole financial system. The smartest people in finance, armed with Nobel-winning models, had been destroyed not by bad analysis but by leverage that left no room to survive being temporarily wrong. It remains the industry's most instructive disaster.

2000. Two very different milestones. Julian Robertson closed Tiger Management after the fund struggled, having refused to chase the technology stocks of the dot-com bubble that then collapsed shortly after. And David Swensen published Pioneering Portfolio Management, the book that laid out the Yale endowment model and inspired a wave of institutions to remake their portfolios around alternatives. The dot-com crash that unfolded this year also validated managers, like Robertson, who had resisted the mania.

2002. As the dot-com wreckage settled, quantitative and systematic strategies gained ground, and firms like Renaissance demonstrated that mathematical approaches could thrive in conditions that punished conventional investors.

2004. The hedge fund industry crossed roughly a trillion dollars in assets, a milestone that marked its transformation from a niche corner of finance into a central force, drawing pension funds, endowments, and institutions that had once kept their distance.

2006. Amaranth Advisors collapsed in one of the fastest large blowups ever. A single trader, Brian Hunter, had made enormous concentrated bets on natural gas prices, positions so large the fund effectively controlled a huge share of the market. When gas prices moved against him, the fund lost roughly 6 billion dollars in weeks and shut down, a stark lesson in the danger of concentration and the ruin that ignoring position limits can bring.

2007. In August, the quant quake struck. Many of the largest quantitative funds suffered severe, simultaneous losses, and the strangest part was that nothing visible in the broader market explained it. The cause was hidden crowding: many funds were running similar strategies holding similar positions, and when one began selling, the forced unwinding cascaded through everyone at once. The event revealed that strategies which appear independent can be dangerously correlated when they rest on the same mathematics. That same year, a handful of managers, most famously John Paulson, made historic profits betting against the subprime mortgage market as the housing bubble began to crack.

2008. The year that tested everything. The financial crisis convulsed global markets, and hedge funds felt it from every direction. Lehman Brothers collapsed in September, freezing the assets of funds that had trusted it as their prime broker and teaching a permanent lesson about counterparty risk. Regulators temporarily banned short selling of many financial stocks, destroying the hedges that convertible arbitrage and other strategies depended on. Volkswagen briefly became the most valuable company in the world in October when a short squeeze trapped funds betting against it. Endowments heavy with illiquid alternatives, including Yale and Harvard, suffered enormous losses and scrambled for cash. Many funds slammed their redemption gates shut, trapping investors' money and traumatizing the industry. And in December, Bernie Madoff was arrested, exposing the largest Ponzi scheme in history, a fraud whose impossibly smooth returns had seduced thousands of sophisticated investors who skipped the basic operational checks that would have revealed it. Amid the carnage, trend-following managed futures funds had one of their best years ever, riding the sustained downward moves that crush other strategies.

2010. In response to the crisis, Congress passed the Dodd-Frank Act, which closed the loophole that had let most hedge fund managers avoid registration and required those overseeing more than 150 million dollars to register with the SEC and submit to examination. The industry was pulled meaningfully further into regulatory daylight.

2013. New rules stemming from the JOBS Act allowed hedge funds, for the first time, to advertise publicly under a provision requiring that all investors be verified as accredited. After decades of enforced silence, funds gained a path to market themselves openly, though many stuck with the quieter traditional approach.

2016. Paul Singer's Elliott Management finally won its long war against Argentina, which settled its defaulted sovereign debt after more than a decade of legal combat that had once included persuading a court in Ghana to detain an Argentine naval ship. The saga captured the distressed investor's defining willingness to fight and wait far longer than anyone else.

2017. Warren Buffett won a ten-year, million-dollar bet he had made against a fund-of-funds firm, Protégé Partners, in 2008. He had wagered that a simple, cheap S&P 500 index fund would beat a basket of hedge funds over the decade, and it did, handily. The outcome became a rallying point for critics who argued that hedge fund fees weren't worth what investors paid.

2018. Two merger arbitrage sagas resolved in opposite directions. A court allowed AT&T's acquisition of Time Warner to proceed despite the government's antitrust challenge, rewarding arbitrageurs who had bet on completion. But the government blocked Broadcom's attempt to buy Qualcomm on national security grounds, killing that deal entirely and punishing anyone positioned for it.

2020. The COVID-19 pandemic triggered a violent market crash in the spring, testing funds under sudden, extreme stress. That same year, the SEC expanded the definition of an accredited investor to include people holding certain financial licenses, the first meaningful acknowledgment that sophistication might come from expertise rather than wealth alone.

2021. A wild year for short sellers. In January, a crowd of individual investors coordinating online deliberately triggered a short squeeze in GameStop, a heavily shorted retailer, sending the stock from a few dollars to hundreds and inflicting billions in losses on the hedge funds short the stock. Melvin Capital, one of the most prominent, was wounded so badly it required a cash injection to survive the month. Then in March, Archegos Capital Management collapsed, having built enormous hidden leverage through swaps arranged separately with multiple banks, none of which could see its total exposure. When its concentrated stocks fell, the forced unwinding inflicted staggering losses on the banks, with Credit Suisse alone losing roughly 5.5 billion dollars. The episode combined hidden leverage and counterparty risk into a single spectacular failure.

2022. Melvin Capital, unable to recover from its GameStop losses, shut down. The broader year brought a sharp inflation shock and aggressive interest rate increases that produced one of the worst years in the history of the bond market, punishing investors caught holding bonds while rewarding trend-following funds that rode the sustained moves in bonds and commodities to a standout year.

2023. After more than a year of fierce regulatory opposition on both sides of the Atlantic, Microsoft's acquisition of the video game company Activision Blizzard finally closed in October. Arbitrageurs who had studied the regulatory arguments and held their positions through months of frightening headlines collected a substantial profit, while the doubters who sold missed it.

The 2020s onward. The industry now manages well over 4 trillion dollars, a scale unimaginable in Jones's era. Machine learning and alternative data have grown from novelties into central tools for quantitative funds, while fees have softened from the rigid 2-and-20 that once defined the business. The debates that ran through this whole history remain unsettled: whether the fees are worth it, whether skill or luck explains the winners, and whether the returns justify the risks. What hasn't changed is the core tension Jones embodied in 1949, the pursuit of returns that behave differently from the market, and the constant danger that the leverage and complexity used to chase them will destroy the people who forget how badly things can go wrong.

Interview Guide to Hedge Funds Across Investment Styles

If you want a job at a hedge fund, you have to walk into a room and prove, in an hour or two, that you think like the people already there. This guide prepares you for that. It's organized by investment style, because a long/short interview and a quant interview test almost entirely different things, and walking in prepared for the wrong one is a fast way to lose the seat.

Two things get judged in every hedge fund interview, and it helps to hold them separate in your mind. The first is knowledge: do you understand how this specific strategy makes money, what its risks are, and why it works? The second, and the more important one, is how you think: can you reason through a problem out loud, can you defend a view under pressure, and can you admit what you don't know without falling apart? Funds can teach you the mechanics of their strategy. They can't easily teach you to think clearly, so that's what they're really screening for. A candidate who reasons well through an unfamiliar problem beats one who memorized answers to familiar ones.

A word on mindset before the specifics. The people interviewing you make their living being wrong a lot and surviving it, so they respect intellectual honesty far more than false confidence. When you don't know something, say so and then reason toward an answer rather than bluffing. When you have a view, hold it firmly enough to defend but loosely enough to update when someone hands you a better argument. That combination, conviction paired with the willingness to change your mind, is exactly what these funds prize in their traders, and demonstrating it in the interview is worth more than any fact you could recite.

What Every Hedge Fund Interview Tests

Before the style-specific material, understand the questions that show up almost everywhere, because they establish whether you can think about investing at all.

The most common opening across fundamental funds is some version of "pitch me an idea." You'll be asked to present a stock, a trade, or an investment you find compelling, and how you handle this single request matters more than anything else in a fundamental interview. It's the whole job compressed into five minutes. Get comfortable with it and much of the rest takes care of itself.

A strong pitch has a clear structure, and you should internalize it until it's automatic. Start with the recommendation and the thesis in one or two sentences, so the interviewer knows immediately what you're arguing. Then explain why the opportunity exists: what does the market believe that you think is wrong, and why is it wrong? This is the heart of any pitch, because a good investment requires a reason the price is mispriced, not just a reason the company is good. A great company at a fair price isn't an opportunity; a misunderstood company at the wrong price is. Next, give the catalyst, the specific event or development that will force the market to see what you see, because a view with no catalyst is an opinion with no timeline. Then, and candidates forget this constantly, lay out the risks and what would prove you wrong. Ending a pitch by naming the ways it could fail signals maturity, while a pitch presented as a sure thing signals the opposite.

Here's the anatomy of a pitch, which you can use as a checklist while you prepare.

Element	What to Say	Why It Matters
Recommendation	The trade and the thesis in one or two sentences	Shows you can lead with the point
Variant view	What the market believes and why it's wrong	This is the actual edge, and the hardest part
Catalyst	The event that will close the gap	Proves you've thought about timing, not just value
Risks	What would make you wrong	Signals maturity and honesty
Sizing	How much conviction the position deserves	Shows you think about downside, not just upside

Beyond the pitch, a few universal questions recur. Expect "where do returns come from?" in some form, because funds want to know you understand the difference between genuine skill and simply riding the market, the distinction between alpha and beta that runs through the book. A candidate who grasps that most returns can be explained by market exposure or well-known factors, and that real skill is the part left over, is already ahead of most applicants.

Expect questions about risk, because every fund cares whether you think about how a trade could hurt you, not just how it could pay. And expect behavioral questions about a time you were wrong, because how you handle being wrong is a genuine predictor of whether you'll survive in this business. Have a real example ready, one where you made an actual mistake, took the loss, and learned something, told without excuses.

Long/Short Equity Interviews

Long/short funds hire people who can find good longs and, harder, good shorts, so the interview centers almost entirely on stock picking and how you think about a portfolio's market exposure.

The stock pitch dominates these interviews, and you should walk in with at least two you can defend cold: a long and, if you can manage it, a short. Preparing a short is where you separate yourself, because most candidates pitch a long they've read about somewhere and freeze when asked to argue the other direction. A strong short pitch names something specifically wrong with a company, fading demand, a business model being destroyed by a competitor, a balance sheet buckling under debt, accounting that doesn't hold together, and pairs it with a catalyst that will expose the problem. Saying a stock is "overvalued" isn't a short thesis and interviewers know it, because expensive stocks can stay expensive for years. If you can walk an interviewer through a genuine short, with a real problem and a real catalyst, you've demonstrated the rarer half of the skill the fund is buying.

Expect to be challenged on your pitch, and welcome it rather than defending reflexively. The interviewer will push back, offer the opposite view, and probe your assumptions, and this is a test of how you handle disagreement, not an attempt to prove you wrong. The best response is to engage seriously, concede points that are genuinely good, and hold your ground where you have real support, showing that you can reason under pressure and update when the evidence warrants. A candidate who crumbles at the first pushback, or who digs in stubbornly against a good argument, fails this test. One who thinks out loud, weighs the challenge honestly, and either strengthens or adjusts the view passes it.

You should understand exposure well enough to discuss it intelligently, because it reveals whether you grasp what a long/short fund actually does. Be ready to explain net exposure, longs minus shorts, which measures the fund's directional bet on the market, and gross exposure, longs plus shorts, which measures total risk and the borrowing behind it. If an interviewer asks how you'd construct a portfolio, showing that you'd think about both the individual picks and the overall market exposure demonstrates real understanding. A candidate who talks only about picking good stocks, with no awareness of how the positions combine into net and gross exposure, looks like someone who's read about investing but never thought about running money.

Come with questions of your own, because a long/short interview is also your chance to learn how the fund works and to signal sophistication. Good questions to ask include how the fund thinks about position sizing, how much of the analysts' work makes it into the portfolio, how ideas get generated and vetted, and how the fund manages its shorts given their unlimited downside. Asking how analysts are evaluated, whether on the profit and loss of their ideas or on something softer, tells you a lot about the seat and shows the interviewer you're thinking like someone who'll be accountable for real decisions.

Here's what strong versus weak candidates look like in a long/short interview.

Dimension	Strong Candidate	Weak Candidate
The pitch	Clear thesis, variant view, catalyst, risks	A company they "like" with no real edge

The short	A specific problem plus a catalyst	"Overvalued" with nothing behind it
Under pushback	Engages, concedes good points, holds real ones	Crumbles or stubbornly digs in
Exposure	Understands net and gross and portfolio construction	Talks only about picking stocks

Global Macro and Managed Futures Interviews

Macro interviews test whether you can connect a view about the world to an actual trade, so they reward candidates who follow markets closely and can reason from economics to a specific position. First, know that macro funds split into two very different kinds, and the interview differs accordingly. A discretionary macro fund wants someone who can form judgments about economies, currencies, and rates and express them through trades, so the interview probes your reasoning about the world. A systematic macro or managed futures fund is closer to a quant shop, wanting mathematical and programming skill, so its interview looks more like the quantitative interviews described later. Figure out which kind you're interviewing with before you prepare.

For a discretionary macro role, expect to be asked for a macro view and a trade to express it. A common question is something like "what's the most interesting thing happening in markets right now, and how would you trade it?" A strong answer connects a specific economic thesis to a specific instrument, explaining not just what you think will happen but why you'd bet on it through this particular trade rather than another. The book showed how one economic view, say that a central bank will raise rates faster than expected, can be expressed through bonds, currencies, or stock index futures, each with a different risk and payoff. A candidate who understands that a view and its expression are separate choices, and who picks the instrument deliberately, demonstrates real macro thinking. One who has a view but no idea how to trade it, or who names a trade with no coherent thesis behind it, hasn't connected the two halves of the job.

Be ready to reason about central banks, because they drive so much of macro. Interviewers may ask what you think a central bank will do next, or how a rate decision would ripple through currencies and bonds. You don't need a certain answer, since nobody has one, but you need to reason through it coherently, showing you understand how rates, currencies, growth, and inflation push against each other. Follow the major central banks and their current debates before any macro interview, because being unable to discuss what the Federal Reserve is currently grappling with is disqualifying for a macro seat.

Prepare to discuss being wrong, because macro punishes stubbornness harder than almost any strategy. In macro, being early looks exactly like being wrong, and a trader who marries a thesis and refuses to abandon it as losses mount can be destroyed even when the eventual call was right. So an interviewer probing how you'd handle a losing macro position is really asking whether you have the discipline to change your mind. The book's account of Long-Term Capital Management, brilliant people ruined because their positions couldn't survive being temporarily wrong, is worth having in mind. A candidate who talks about cutting losses, respecting the market's verdict, and staying flexible understands something that many smart people never learn.

Event-Driven and Relative Value Interviews

Event-driven interviews test whether you can assess the probability of a specific corporate event and whether you understand the asymmetric payoff that defines these strategies, so they reward precision and a respect for downside. The defining feature to demonstrate, as the book stressed, is an understanding that these strategies produce frequent small gains punctuated by rare large losses. A candidate who talks only about the gains, without showing awareness of the severe downside when an event breaks the wrong way, has missed the essence of the strategy.

For a merger arbitrage role, be ready to analyze a live deal or a hypothetical one. You might be asked to walk through how you'd evaluate whether an announced merger will close, and a strong answer reveals understanding of why deals break: antitrust review, financing failure, shareholder rejection, material adverse change clauses. Being able to compute a deal spread and annualize it, buy the target at its current price, capture the gap to the offer price if it closes, and translate that into an annualized return, shows you grasp the mechanics. But the more impressive thing is showing you understand the asymmetry: the upside is capped at the small spread while the downside from a broken deal is large, so the whole game is assessing the probability of completion accurately. A candidate who can discuss a real deal, like the year-plus regulatory fight over Microsoft's acquisition of Activision Blizzard, and reason about how they'd have handled holding through the frightening headlines, demonstrates exactly the judgment these funds hire for.

For a distressed or credit role, you need to understand the priority of claims cold, because it's the foundation of the entire strategy. Be ready to explain the bankruptcy waterfall, the strict order in which claims get paid when a company fails, from secured creditors at the top down to common shareholders at the bottom who almost always get wiped out. Understanding the concept of the fulcrum security, the layer of debt where a company's value runs out and whose holders often convert into ownership of the reorganized company, signals that you grasp where the real skill in distressed investing lies. If you can discuss the difference between reorganization, where the company survives and restructures, and liquidation, where it shuts down and sells its assets, and how each affects recovery values, you're speaking the language of the desk. These interviews also probe temperament, because distressed investing demands patience through long, messy, drawn-out situations, so being able to discuss why you'd have the stomach for a multi-year bankruptcy fight matters.

For relative value and arbitrage roles, expect questions about the relationships you'd trade and what could break them. The book's example of the 2005 General Motors episode, where a supposedly safe trade of long GM bonds and short GM stock blew up when two unexpected events hit both legs in opposite directions, is the cautionary tale to reference. A strong candidate understands that the relationships these strategies rely on can shatter under unforeseen events, and can reason about what those events might be. Understanding the role of borrowing is also important, because relative value strategies typically amplify small mispricings with large amounts of borrowed money, and the 2008 collapse of convertible arbitrage showed how strategies that look low-risk can unravel violently when borrowing and short selling both vanish at once. Showing that you understand this fragility, rather than treating arbitrage as free money, marks you as someone who's actually thought about the risks.

Quantitative and Systematic Interviews

Quant interviews are a different animal entirely, testing mathematics, statistics, probability, programming, and clear technical reasoning rather than investment judgment, so they demand a different kind of preparation. If you're interviewing for a quant role, the process will likely include technical problems solved on the spot: probability puzzles, statistics questions, math problems, and coding challenges. These test raw analytical horsepower and the ability to reason precisely under pressure, and there's no substitute for practicing them beforehand. Candidates who haven't drilled probability and coding problems get exposed immediately, because these interviews move fast and expect fluency.

The conceptual understanding that separates strong quant candidates centers on overfitting, the trap the book examined at length. Expect to discuss how you'd know whether a pattern in data is real or just noise, and a strong answer covers out-of-sample testing, holding out data the model was never trained on, keeping models simple enough to avoid fitting noise, and demanding a genuine economic rationale for why a pattern should persist. Showing that you'd treat a beautiful backtest with suspicion rather than excitement, because a backtest can be tuned to look as good as you want, demonstrates the single most important instinct in quantitative investing. A candidate who's impressed by strong historical simulations, rather than wary of them, reveals a dangerous naivety that would worry any serious quant.

Be prepared to discuss the practical dangers that come up in real quant work, because they show you understand the field beyond the textbook. Crowding is one: the 2007 quant quake, where many funds running similar strategies suffered simultaneous losses as forced selling cascaded through crowded trades, revealed that strategies appearing independent can be dangerously correlated when everyone runs the same mathematics on the same data. Showing awareness that a profitable pattern erodes as more people trade it, and that popularity is itself a risk, marks sophistication.

The interpretability of complex models is another – some machine learning models become black boxes whose decisions even their creators can't fully explain, and being able to discuss the trade-off between a model's predictive power and the ability to understand what it's doing signals that you've thought about a real problem the field wrestles with.

Here's how to prepare for the different demands of a quant interview.

Area	What to Expect	How to Prepare
Probability and math	Puzzles and problems solved live	Drill problem sets until fluent
Coding	Write and reason about code on the spot	Practice in the language the fund uses
Overfitting	Conceptual questions on real vs. noise	Understand out-of-sample testing deeply
Statistics	Questions on inference and modeling	Review the fundamentals cold
Markets	Lighter than fundamental interviews	Know the basics, don't neglect entirely

One caution specific to quant roles. Even at heavily technical funds, don't neglect a basic understanding of markets, because the best quant firms want people who connect their mathematics to real economic behavior rather than treating markets as an abstract dataset. Being able to explain why a pattern might exist, tying it to how investors actually behave, distinguishes a candidate who understands investing from one who only understands statistics. The strongest quant hires tend to have both.

Activist Investing Interviews

Activist funds hire people who can diagnose what's wrong with a company and prescribe a fix, then think through how to force that fix on resistant management, so the interview combines deep fundamental analysis with strategic thinking about corporate change. Expect to be asked to analyze a company and identify what an activist could do to improve it. A strong answer diagnoses a specific problem, a bloated cost structure, a misguided strategy, a division that should be sold, poor capital allocation, and prescribes a concrete plan to fix it. Vague observations that a company is "underperforming," without a specific remedy, show you haven't done the analytical work activism requires. The best candidates can look at a company and articulate exactly what they'd change and why it would create value.

The harder part, and what separates activist thinking from ordinary stock analysis, is the campaign itself. Owning a stake and having good ideas accomplishes nothing if you can't force change, so be ready to discuss how you'd actually make it happen when management resists. This means understanding the mechanics of a proxy fight, a campaign to win board seats by persuading other shareholders to vote with you, and understanding that an activist's power comes entirely from convincing the broader shareholder base to agree. A candidate who grasps that activism is as much about persuasion and coalition-building as about analysis understands the full nature of the work.

Show that you can think about whether an intervention helps or harms a company over the long run, because it's the central debate about activism and interviewers respect candidates who engage with it honestly. Some activist campaigns impose useful discipline on complacent management; others push for buybacks and cost cuts that lift the stock for a few quarters while damaging the business's future. Being able to discuss this tension, and to distinguish value creation from short-term financial engineering, demonstrates maturity. The book's example of Bill Ackman's roughly billion-dollar loss shorting Herbalife is worth referencing as a reminder that activism, especially on the short side, pits you against a living company that fights back, against other investors who may take the opposite side, and against the possibility that you're simply wrong.

Demonstrating You Understand Risk

Whatever style you're interviewing for, weaving risk awareness through your answers will set you apart, because the book's central lesson holds across every strategy: most funds that die don't die from bad investing but from failing to survive being wrong. Interviewers notice when a candidate thinks naturally about downside, and they worry about candidates who talk only about how trades will make money.

The habit to build is naming the risks in every idea you present, unprompted. When you pitch a trade, end with what would make you wrong and how much you could lose, because volunteering the downside signals that you understand investing is about managing risk, not just finding winners. This applies to the pitch, to any hypothetical you're handed, and to how you discuss markets generally. A candidate who reflexively considers what could go wrong sounds like someone who'd survive, while one who sees only upside sounds like someone who'd blow up.

Understand position sizing and concentration well enough to discuss them, because they're where risk management becomes concrete. The book showed how the collapse of Amaranth, which lost roughly six billion dollars on a single concentrated natural gas bet, illustrates that even a plausible thesis can destroy a fund when the position is too large. Showing that you'd think about how much to bet on any single idea, sizing it so that being wrong is survivable rather than fatal, demonstrates real understanding. Being able to reference how leverage magnifies both gains and losses, and how it destroyed Long-Term Capital Management by leaving no room to endure being temporarily wrong, shows you've absorbed the hardest lesson in the field.

Talk about correlation and how it behaves under stress, because it's a subtle risk that impresses interviewers when a candidate raises it. The book explained how correlations spike toward one in a crisis, so a portfolio that looks diversified in calm times can turn out to be a single concentrated bet on market stability, as LTCM discovered. A candidate who understands that comfortable correlations can vanish exactly when protection is needed most is thinking at a level above the typical applicant.

Questions You Should Ask Them

An interview runs both ways, and the questions you ask reveal your sophistication while helping you judge whether the fund is a place you actually want to work. Prepared candidates always have thoughtful questions, and having none signals a lack of seriousness. Beyond making a good impression, these questions help you evaluate the seat, because not every fund is a good place to build a career, and the interview is your chance to find out.

Ask about the work itself and how ideas flow. Good questions include how ideas get generated and vetted, how much of an analyst's research actually reaches the portfolio, and how decisions get made when the analyst and the portfolio manager disagree. The answers tell you whether you'd have real influence or simply feed research to someone who ignores it, which matters enormously for your growth. Asking how analysts are evaluated, whether on the measured profit and loss of their ideas or on something less defined, reveals how accountable and how visible your work would be.

Ask about the fund's edge and its thinking on risk, because these questions show you understand what matters and help you assess whether the fund is any good. Asking what the fund believes its durable advantage is, and how it thinks about the risk of that edge eroding as others copy it, signals that you grasp how strategies decay over time. Asking how the fund manages risk and what scenarios worry the people running it tells you whether risk is taken seriously or treated as an afterthought, which is a genuine predictor of whether the fund will still exist in a decade.

Here are questions worth asking versus ones that fall flat.

Strong Questions to Ask	Weak Questions to Ask
How does an idea travel from analyst to portfolio?	What are the hours like?
How are analysts evaluated and given more responsibility?	How much vacation do I get?
What does the fund see as its durable edge?	Anything easily answered by the fund's website
How does the fund think about risk and what worries it?	Nothing, or purely generic questions
How do the analyst and PM resolve disagreement?	Questions that show you didn't research the fund

Be thoughtful about compensation questions, because there's a right time and a wrong way to raise them. Early interviews aren't the place to lead with pay, but understanding how compensation works at the fund, whether analysts share in the performance of their ideas, matters for your career and is fair to explore as the process advances. How a fund structures pay reveals how it thinks about aligning your interests with its results, the same alignment principle the book applied to managers and their investors.

How to Prepare

Walking into a hedge fund interview underprepared is obvious within minutes, so serious preparation is what earns you the seat. The specifics vary by style, but the discipline is the same: know the strategy, know your own material cold, and know the particular fund.

For fundamental roles, long/short, event-driven, activist, the single most important preparation is your investment ideas. Have at least two or three you can present and defend without notes, each with a clear thesis, a variant view, a catalyst, and the risks that would prove you wrong. Practice pitching them out loud, ideally to someone who'll push back, because the ability to present an idea smoothly and then defend it under challenge is exactly what these interviews test. A polished pitch that falls apart under the first question is worse than no pitch at all, so rehearse the defense as much as the pitch itself.

For quant roles, drill the technical material relentlessly, because these interviews expect fluency in probability, statistics, and coding that only practice produces. Work through problem sets, practice coding in the language the fund uses, and make sure you can reason about overfitting and model validation clearly. The conceptual understanding matters alongside the raw problem-solving, so be ready to discuss why a good backtest proves little and how you'd distinguish a real pattern from noise.

Know the specific fund before you walk in, because generic preparation reads as indifference. Understand the fund's strategy, its history, and anything public about how it invests, and shape your answers to fit. Pitching a long-only value idea to a fund known for aggressive shorting, or a discretionary macro view to a systematic shop, shows you didn't do your homework. Tailoring your ideas and your questions to what the fund actually does signals genuine interest and the kind of diligence the job itself demands.

Finally, know your own resume cold, because interviewers will probe every claim on it. Be ready to discuss any past work, any investment you've made, any project you've listed, in real depth, because a candidate who can't defend their own stated experience raises immediate doubts. Even skills and interests. If you put Spanish as one of your skills, they could very well find a native speaker on staff to test that claim. If you claim to follow markets, be ready to discuss what's happening in them right now, because nothing sinks a candidate faster than professing passion for investing and then being unable to name a single thing they find interesting in the current market.

What Interviewers Are Really Looking For

Underneath the specific questions, interviewers are assessing a handful of qualities that predict whether you'll succeed, and understanding these helps you present yourself well across any style of fund.

Clarity of thought comes first. The people interviewing you value the ability to take something complicated and explain it simply, to reason through a problem step by step, and to communicate a view without hiding behind jargon. A candidate who thinks clearly and speaks clearly stands out immediately, because clear communication reflects clear thinking, and clear thinking is the whole job. Practice explaining your ideas in plain language, because dressing up a simple point in complexity makes you sound like you don't understand it.

Intellectual honesty is prized more highly in this field than in almost any other, because the entire business runs on assessing reality accurately rather than telling comforting stories. Admitting what you don't know, conceding a good argument, and discussing your own mistakes openly all signal the honesty these funds depend on. A candidate who bluffs, who can't acknowledge a strong counterpoint, or who claims to have never really been wrong triggers suspicion, because everyone in the room knows that being wrong is constant and that people who can't admit it are dangerous. Paradoxically, showing you can be wrong gracefully makes you look more capable, not less.

Genuine curiosity about markets and the willingness to keep learning round out what interviewers seek. The best people in this business are relentlessly curious, following markets because they find them fascinating rather than because they have to, and that curiosity shows in an interview. A candidate who lights up discussing an interesting situation, who has clearly been thinking about markets on their own, and who asks sharp questions out of real interest conveys something no amount of preparation can fake. Combined with the clear thinking and intellectual honesty already described, it presents the picture every hedge fund wants to hire: someone who thinks well, tells the truth, manages risk, and genuinely wants to understand how markets work.

Whichever style you pursue and whichever side of the table you eventually sit on, the goal of your preparation is the same: to understand a strategy deeply enough to explain how it makes money, where its edge comes from, and what would make it fail. Master that, present it clearly, and stay honest about the limits of what you know, and you'll have shown the clear thinking that this field, for all its complexity, ultimately rewards.

Key Terms and Definitions

- **Absolute return** - A strategy goal of earning positive returns regardless of whether the broader market rises or falls. The target is making money in any environment rather than beating an index.
- **Accredited investor** - An individual who meets wealth or income thresholds, or holds certain financial licenses, and is therefore permitted to invest in most private funds. The thresholds are a rough proxy for the ability to bear risk.
- **Activist investing** - A strategy in which an investor buys a large stake in a company and pushes for changes, such as new management or a sale, to lift the stock. Power comes from persuading other shareholders to agree.
- **Alpha** - The portion of an investment's return that comes from skill or something specific to the holding, rather than from the market's overall movement. It's the part a manager can genuinely claim credit for.
- **Alternative data** - Unconventional information sources, like satellite images or credit card transactions, that quantitative funds analyze for predictive signals. It extends investing far beyond traditional financial statements.
- **Alternative investment** - Any investment outside traditional stocks, bonds, and cash, including hedge funds, private equity, real estate, and commodities. Defined by lighter regulation, restricted access, and lower liquidity.
- **Backfill bias** - The distortion created when funds report their returns to a database only after building a good record, then add that strong history retroactively. It inflates reported industry returns.
- **Backtesting** - Simulating how a strategy would have performed by applying its rules to historical data. Useful for evaluation but dangerously easy to abuse.
- **Beta** - The portion of an investment's return that comes from moving with the overall market. It can be obtained cheaply through an index fund and doesn't justify high fees.
- **Borrow cost** - The fee charged for borrowing shares to short them, quoted as an annual rate. Hard-to-borrow stocks can carry very high costs that erode a short position.
- **Capital call** - A demand from a private fund for an investor to provide committed capital, arriving on the fund's schedule rather than the investor's. Unmet needs for cash to meet capital calls can strain an institution.
- **Capital structure arbitrage** - Betting on inconsistencies between different securities issued by the same company, such as its stock and its bonds. Profits come when the misaligned prices return to a sensible relationship.
- **Carried interest** - The performance share a fund's general partner receives, often taxed as a capital gain rather than as ordinary income. Its favorable tax treatment is a longstanding source of controversy.
- **Carry trade** - Borrowing in a low-interest-rate currency and investing in a high-interest-rate one to capture the difference. It produces steady gains until volatility triggers sudden, sharp losses.

- **Catalyst** - A specific event expected to force the market to recognize what an investor already sees, such as an earnings miss or a regulatory ruling. A short thesis without a catalyst is just an opinion with no timeline.
- **Chapter 11** - A bankruptcy process that lets a company restructure its debts and keep operating rather than shutting down. It's where loan-to-own distressed strategies play out.
- **Chapter 7** - A bankruptcy process in which a company shuts down entirely and its assets are sold off and distributed to creditors. It's liquidation rather than reorganization.
- **Concentration limit** - A rule capping how much of a portfolio can be exposed to any single position, sector, or theme. It ensures no single bad bet can destroy the fund.
- **Conditional Value at Risk (Expected Shortfall)** - A risk measure showing the average loss on the bad days when losses exceed the Value at Risk threshold. It captures the severity of extreme outcomes that plain VaR ignores.
- **Convertible arbitrage** - Buying a convertible bond and shorting the underlying stock to profit from the bond's mispriced conversion option and the stock's volatility. It relies heavily on borrowing and short selling.
- **Convertible bond** - A bond that the holder can convert into a set number of the company's shares. It behaves as both a bond and an option on the stock.
- **Correlation** - A measure of how closely two investments move together, ranging from moving identically to moving oppositely. Combining assets with low correlation reduces portfolio risk.
- **Counterparty risk** - The risk that a firm you depend on, such as a broker or trading partner, fails and harms you even if your own decisions were sound. It runs in both directions between a fund and its counterparties.
- **CTA (Commodity Trading Advisor)** - A regulatory label for funds that trade futures contracts systematically, despite the outdated name they trade far more than commodities. Most run trend-following strategies.
- **Data mining** - Searching through enough data and strategies that something appears profitable by pure chance. Reporting only the strategies that worked mistakes luck for discovery.
- **Deal spread** - The gap between a target company's stock price and the price an acquirer has agreed to pay. It reflects the market's doubt that the deal will close.
- **Delta hedging** - Continuously adjusting the size of a short position as the underlying stock moves, central to convertible arbitrage. It lets a manager profit from volatility regardless of direction.
- **Discretionary trading** - An approach in which a human makes each decision using judgment and experience. It adapts well to novel events but carries emotional and key-person risk.
- **Distressed debt** - The bonds and loans of troubled companies, trading at steep discounts because the market doubts full repayment. Investors buy them betting the recovery exceeds the depressed price.
- **Dodd-Frank Act** - A 2010 law passed after the financial crisis that, among many provisions, required most large hedge fund managers to register with the SEC. It pulled the industry further into regulatory oversight.
- **Efficient frontier** - The set of portfolios offering the highest return for each level of risk. Building a portfolio on the frontier means taking no more risk than necessary for its return.

- **Endowment model** - The approach pioneered by David Swensen at Yale, emphasizing heavy allocation to illiquid alternatives and access to elite managers. It relies on a long horizon and advantages that are hard to copy.
- **ESG** - Environmental, social, and governance factors that investors increasingly weigh alongside financial results. Its role in investing is genuinely contested.
- **Event-driven** - Strategies that profit from specific corporate events like mergers, bankruptcies, and spin-offs. Returns depend on whether a defined event happens rather than on market direction.
- **Expected shortfall** - See Conditional Value at Risk.
- **Factor investing** - Building portfolios around characteristics, like value or momentum, that have historically been associated with higher returns. These factors can often be captured cheaply.
- **Fat tails** - The tendency of financial markets to produce extreme events far more often than a normal bell curve predicts. Models built on the bell curve badly understate the risk of disaster.
- **Fulcrum security** - The layer of a company's debt where its value runs out in bankruptcy, whose holders often convert their claims into ownership. Identifying it is the central skill in distressed investing.
- **Fund-of-funds** - A fund that invests in a portfolio of other hedge funds, offering diversification and professional selection. Its main drawback is an extra layer of fees stacked on the underlying funds.
- **Fundamental analysis** - The work of estimating what a company is truly worth by studying its financials, industry, and management. It underpins stock selection in long/short investing.
- **Gate** - A restriction limiting how much investors can withdraw from a fund in a single period. Funds impose gates to prevent a stampede of redemptions from forcing damaging sales.
- **General partner (GP)** - The entity that runs a fund, makes its investment decisions, and bears legal responsibility. It's usually a company set up to shield the actual managers from unlimited liability.
- **Global macro** - A strategy that bets on the direction of entire economies, currencies, interest rates, and commodities. It works from the top down, starting with the largest economic forces.
- **Gross exposure** - The total size of a fund's positions, longs and shorts added together, ignoring direction. It reveals how much borrowing and total risk the fund carries.
- **Hard hurdle** - A hurdle rate under which the performance fee applies only to returns above the hurdle. It's more favorable to investors than a soft hurdle.
- **High-water mark** - The highest value an investor's account has previously reached, above which performance fees resume. It ensures investors never pay a performance fee twice for the same gains.
- **Hurdle rate** - A minimum return a fund must clear before it can charge a performance fee. It prevents managers from earning fees on returns investors could have gotten with no skill.
- **Illiquidity premium** - The extra expected return that compensates investors for locking up their money in hard-to-sell investments. It's real but only materializes if the manager delivers.
- **Impact investing** - Investing that seeks measurable social or environmental results alongside financial return. It sometimes accepts lower returns in exchange for real-world effect.

- **Investment Advisers Act of 1940** - The law governing investment advisers, including many hedge fund managers. Dodd-Frank later required more of them to register under it.
- **Investment Company Act of 1940** - The strict law governing pooled investment vehicles like mutual funds. Hedge funds arrange themselves to fall outside its definition of an investment company.
- **Kelly criterion** - A formula for the optimal bet size based on your edge and the odds you face. It shows that bet size should scale with your advantage while always leaving room to survive.
- **Key-person risk** - The danger that a fund depends entirely on one irreplaceable individual. If that person leaves, falls ill, or falters, the whole fund is jeopardized.
- **Leverage** - The use of borrowed money to increase the size of an investment. It magnifies both gains and losses, and it has destroyed many funds that used too much.
- **Limited partner (LP)** - An investor in a fund who supplies capital but has no say in its management. Liability is limited to the amount invested.
- **Loan-to-own** - A distressed strategy of buying a company's fulcrum debt intending to convert it into ownership when the company reorganizes. The investor buys debt but ends up controlling the business.
- **Lock-up period** - An initial stretch after investing during which an investor cannot withdraw. It lets the manager invest with a longer horizon without fearing sudden redemptions.
- **Managed futures** - Strategies, usually run by CTAs, that trade futures contracts systematically, most often through trend-following. They tend to profit during market crashes.
- **Management fee** - An annual fee charged on the total assets invested, regardless of performance. At large funds it becomes an enormous guaranteed profit stream on its own.
- **Margin call** - A lender's demand that a borrower post more collateral after positions lose value. It can force a leveraged fund to sell into a falling market, deepening its losses.
- **Market neutral** - A portfolio balanced so its longs and shorts offset the market's direction, leaving near-zero net exposure. Its returns come from stock selection rather than market movement.
- **Master-feeder structure** - An arrangement in which onshore and offshore feeder funds pool their money into a single master fund where all trading occurs. It serves investors with different tax situations efficiently.
- **Mean reversion** - The tendency of prices to return to an average level after straying from it. It underlies statistical arbitrage.
- **Merger arbitrage** - Buying a target company after a merger is announced, betting the deal closes and the stock rises to the offer price. The upside is small and capped while the downside from a broken deal is severe.
- **Modern Portfolio Theory** - Harry Markowitz's framework showing that portfolio risk depends on how holdings move together, not just their individual risks. It justifies diversification but strains when applied to alternatives.
- **Momentum factor** - The tendency of stocks that have risen recently to keep rising for a while. It's one of the main documented return factors.
- **Net asset value (NAV)** - The calculated worth of a fund's holdings, ideally computed by an independent administrator. Self-calculation of NAV is a major fraud red flag.

- **Net exposure** - A fund's directional bet on the market, calculated as longs minus shorts. It reveals how much the fund will move with the market.
- **Offshore fund** - A fund registered in a foreign jurisdiction like the Cayman Islands, serving non-U.S. and U.S. tax-exempt investors. It helps tax-exempt institutions avoid an adverse tax on borrowed-money profits.
- **Onshore fund** - A domestic fund, typically a Delaware limited partnership, serving U.S. taxable investors. Its pass-through structure suits taxable Americans.
- **Operational due diligence** - The investigation of everything about a fund other than its strategy, including who holds the assets and who audits the books. It catches the operational failures behind many fund collapses.
- **Out-of-sample testing** - Testing a strategy on data it wasn't built with, to see whether it still works. It's the main defense against overfitting.
- **Overfitting** - Tuning a strategy so precisely to historical data that it captures random noise rather than real patterns. It produces beautiful backtests that fail with real money.
- **Pair trading** - Buying one stock and shorting a similar one when their normal relationship stretches abnormally. Profit comes from the two converging, independent of the market.
- **Performance fee** - The share of profits a manager collects, often 20 percent, that aligns her interests with investors. Also called the incentive fee or carried interest.
- **Position sizing** - Deciding how much to invest in any single position so that no bet can inflict fatal damage. It balances conviction against survival.
- **Prime broker** - A large bank that lends a hedge fund money and securities, holds its assets, and clears its trades. A fund is deeply dependent on its prime broker's health.
- **Priority of claims (absolute priority rule)** - The strict order in which claims get paid when a company fails, from secured creditors down to common shareholders. It determines which distressed securities recover value.
- **Proxy fight** - A campaign by an activist to win seats on a company's board by persuading shareholders to vote for her nominees. It's the escalation when management resists.
- **Qualified purchaser** - An investor meeting a high threshold, generally five million dollars in investments, permitted to invest in funds that accept unlimited such investors. It's a steeper bar than accredited investor status.
- **Rehypothecation** - A prime broker's reuse of a client's collateral for its own purposes. When Lehman collapsed, rehypothecated assets became entangled in the bankruptcy and hard to recover.
- **Relative return** - Success measured against a benchmark, where beating the index counts as winning even if investors lost money. It's the standard most of the investment industry uses.
- **Short selling** - Borrowing shares, selling them, and later buying them back to profit from a price decline. Its potential loss is unlimited because the stock can rise without limit.
- **Short squeeze** - A feedback loop in which a rising stock forces short sellers to buy back shares, pushing the price higher and trapping more shorts. GameStop in 2021 was a famous example.
- **Side pocket** - A separate account segregating hard-to-sell positions so redeeming investors can't force a fire sale. It protects the fund's remaining investors.

- **Size factor** - The historical tendency of smaller companies to earn higher returns than larger ones. It was one of the first documented factors beyond market risk.
- **Skin in the game** - The amount of a manager's own money invested in her fund on the same terms as outside investors. A large personal stake is the strongest sign of aligned interests.
- **Smart beta** - Low-cost products that systematically capture factor premia like value and momentum. They undercut hedge funds charging premium fees for what is partly factor exposure.
- **Special situations** - A catch-all for unusual corporate events that create temporary mispricings, such as spin-offs and restructurings. The event, not the market, drives the opportunity.
- **Spin-off** - The separation of a division into an independent, publicly traded company, with shares distributed to existing shareholders. Forced selling by uninterested recipients often leaves the new company underpriced.
- **Statistical arbitrage** - Applying mean-reversion trading across thousands of securities using computers, profiting from tiny edges multiplied across many trades. It relies on the law of large numbers.
- **Stress testing** - Estimating how a portfolio would perform under specific bad scenarios rather than statistical probabilities. It catches tail risks that models like VaR miss.
- **Survivorship bias** - The distortion created when failed funds disappear from the data, leaving only survivors. It makes the whole industry look more successful than it was.
- **Systematic trading** - An approach in which computers make every trade according to predefined rules. It applies consistent discipline but can fail when facing genuinely unprecedented events.
- **Total return swap** - A derivative giving an investor the economic exposure of owning an asset without holding it directly. It can hide leverage, as it did in the Archegos collapse.
- **Trend-following** - Betting that markets moving in a sustained direction will keep moving that way, the core strategy of most managed futures. It shines in crises but suffers in choppy, directionless markets.
- **Value at Risk (VaR)** - A measure expressing potential loss as a dollar amount tied to a probability and time period. It's widely used but silent on how bad losses get once its threshold is crossed.
- **Value factor** - The historical tendency of cheap stocks to outperform expensive ones over time. It traces back to the value investing of Benjamin Graham.
- **Whipsaw** - The repeated small losses a trend-following system suffers in a range-bound market, buying just before drops and selling just before rises. It's the strategy's main weakness.

References & Recommended Readings

Works Cited

Ang, A. (2014). *Asset management: A systematic approach to factor investing.* Oxford University Press.

Asness, C. S., Moskowitz, T. J., & Pedersen, L. H. (2013). Value and momentum everywhere. *The Journal of Finance, 68*(3), 929–985.

Bailey, D. H., Borwein, J. M., López de Prado, M., & Zhu, Q. J. (2014). Pseudo-mathematics and financial charlatanism: The effects of backtest overfitting on out-of-sample performance. *Notices of the American Mathematical Society, 61*(5), 458–471.

Black, F., & Scholes, M. (1973). The pricing of options and corporate liabilities. *Journal of Political Economy, 81*(3), 637–654.

Brown, S. J., Goetzmann, W. N., & Ibbotson, R. G. (1999). Offshore hedge funds: Survival and performance, 1989–1995. *The Journal of Business, 72*(1), 91–117.

Covel, M. W. (2009). *The complete TurtleTrader: The legend, the lessons, the results.* HarperBusiness.

Fama, E. F., & French, K. R. (1992). The cross-section of expected stock returns. *The Journal of Finance, 47*(2), 427–465.

Fama, E. F., & French, K. R. (1993). Common risk factors in the returns on stocks and bonds. *Journal of Financial Economics, 33*(1), 3–56.

Financial Crisis Inquiry Commission. (2011). *The financial crisis inquiry report.* U.S. Government Printing Office.

Fung, W., & Hsieh, D. A. (2001). The risk in hedge fund strategies: Theory and evidence from trend followers. *The Review of Financial Studies, 14*(2), 313–341.

Greenblatt, J. (1997). *You can be a stock market genius: Uncover the secret hiding places of stock market profits.* Simon & Schuster.

Ineichen, A. M. (2003). *Absolute returns: The risk and opportunities of hedge fund investing.* John Wiley & Sons.

Jegadeesh, N., & Titman, S. (1993). Returns to buying winners and selling losers: Implications for stock market efficiency. *The Journal of Finance, 48*(1), 65–91.

Jorion, P. (2007). *Value at risk: The new benchmark for managing financial risk* (3rd ed.). McGraw-Hill.

Kelly, J. L. (1956). A new interpretation of information rate. *The Bell System Technical Journal, 35*(4), 917–926.

Khandani, A. E., & Lo, A. W. (2011). What happened to the quants in August 2007? Evidence from factors and transactions data. *Journal of Financial Markets, 14*(1), 1–46.

Lo, A. W. (2008). *Hedge funds: An analytic perspective.* Princeton University Press.

Loomis, C. J. (1966, April). The Jones nobody keeps up with. *Fortune, 73*(4), 237–247.

Lowenstein, R. (2000). *When genius failed: The rise and fall of Long-Term Capital Management.* Random House.

Mallaby, S. (2010). *More money than god: Hedge funds and the making of a new elite.* Penguin Press.

Markopolos, H. (2010). *No one would listen: A true financial thriller.* John Wiley & Sons.

Markowitz, H. (1952). Portfolio selection. *The Journal of Finance, 7*(1), 77–91.

Merton, R. C. (1974). On the pricing of corporate debt: The risk structure of interest rates. *The Journal of Finance, 29*(2), 449–470.

Pedersen, L. H. (2015). *Efficiently inefficient: How smart money invests and market prices are determined.* Princeton University Press.

Sharpe, W. F. (1966). Mutual fund performance. *The Journal of Business, 39*(1), 119–138.

Swensen, D. F. (2009). *Pioneering portfolio management: An unconventional approach to institutional investment* (Rev. ed.). Free Press.

Zuckerman, G. (2019). *The man who solved the market: How Jim Simons launched the quant revolution.* Portfolio/Penguin.

Recommended Readings

Dalio, R. (2018). *Principles for navigating big debt crises.* Bridgewater.

> Dalio lays out the debt-cycle framework that drives his macro thinking. It's the clearest window into how a systematic macro shop actually models the economy.

Drobny, S. (2006). *Inside the house of money: Top hedge fund traders on profiting in the global markets.* John Wiley & Sons.

> A set of candid interviews with global macro traders that shows, in their own words, how they turn an economic view into a real trade.

Lack, S. (2012). *The hedge fund mirage: The illusion of big money and why it's too good to be true.* John Wiley & Sons.

> The sharpest critical take on the industry, arguing that investors as a group have kept far less of the returns than the marketing suggests. Read it to keep yourself honest about fees.

Schwager, J. D. (2012). *Hedge fund market wizards: How winning traders win.* John Wiley & Sons.

> Interviews with successful managers across nearly every style in this book, useful both for the strategy insight and for the recurring emphasis on risk and discipline.

Soros, G. (2003). *The alchemy of finance.* John Wiley & Sons.

> Part memoir, part philosophy from the trader who broke the Bank of England, offering his theory of how markets and participants influence each other.